In search of
Harry Potter

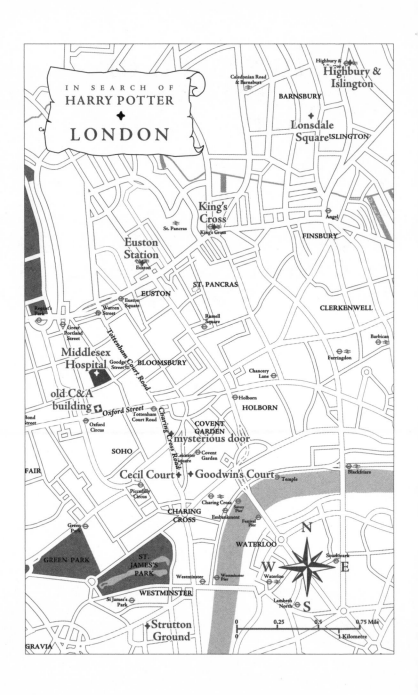

IN SEARCH OF
HARRY POTTER
✦
LONDON

Highbury &
**Highbury &
Islington**
Caledonian Road
& Barnsbury
BARNSBURY
**Lonsdale
Square** ISLINGTON
Angel
**King's
Cross**
St. Pancras
King's Cross
FINSBURY
**Euston
Station**
Euston
ST. PANCRAS
EUSTON
CLERKENWELL
Regent's
Park
Euston
Square
Warren
Street
Russell
Square
Great
Portland
Street
Barbican
**Middlesex
Hospital**
Goodge
Street
BLOOMSBURY
Farringdon
**old C&A
building**
Chancery
Lane
Bond
Street
Oxford Street
Tottenham
Court Road
Holborn
HOLBORN
Oxford
Circus
**COVENT
GARDEN**
mysterious door
SOHO
Leicester
Square
Covent
Garden
MAYFAIR
Blackfriars
Cecil Court ✦ ✦ **Goodwin's Court**
Temple
Piccadilly
Circus
Charing Cross
Savoy
Pier
**CHARING
CROSS**
Embankment
Festival
Pier
Green
Park
WATERLOO
N
GREEN PARK
**ST.
JAMES'S
PARK**
Southwark
Westminster
Westminster
Pier
W Waterloo **E**
St James's
Park
WESTMINSTER
Lambeth
North
S
✦ **Strutton
Ground**
0   0.25   0.5   0.75 Mile
0   1 Kilometre
BELGRAVIA

In search of Harry Potter

✦ ✦ ✦

STEVE VANDER ARK

Methuen

First published in Great Britain by Methuen 2008

Copyright © 2008 by Steve Vander Ark

Copyright in the photographs © 2008 by Steve Vander Ark except as separately acknowledged

Copyright in the maps © 2008 by Camilla Engleby

1 3 5 7 9 10 8 6 4 2

Methuen
8 Artillery Row
London
SW1P 1RZ

www.methuen.co.uk

A CIP catalogue record for this book is available from the British Library

ISBN 13: 978-0-413-77667-9

Printed and bound in Great Britain by
Butler Tanner & Dennis, Frome, Somerset

For my grandfather, Rev. Cornelius Witt,
who inspired a love of travel in his family and in whose study
I discovered the wonders of fantasy literature
in the pages of *A Princess of Mars*.

ACKNOWLEDGEMENTS

Special thanks to travelling companions over the years whose insights and support made the search for Harry Potter not only possible but a lot more fun.

Thanks also to the fans who shared my experiences at conventions and through correspondence, and who encouraged me to undertake this project.

Thanks to Tim Ledbetter for kindly allowing me to include his essays in the book .

Special thanks to Brenda Vander Ark for sharing the adventure to Scotland and for letting me use a couple of her photographs.

Thanks to Camilla Engelby for the beautiful cover and maps, and to Rachael Livermore for her encouragement and assistance with the creation of this book.

Quoditch Moor photographs courtesy Viridian Photography.

Spinner's End photograph courtesy Richard Crawshaw.

Duart Castle photograph courtesy Undiscovered Scotland, www.undiscoveredscotland.co.uk.

Iyer, Pico. The playing fields of Hogwarts. The New York Times Online, 10 October 1999. http://www.nytimes.com/books/99/10/10/bookend/bookend.html

The Proceedings of the Old Bailey, http://www.hrionline.ac.uk/oldbailey/html_units/1730s/t17350702-42.html

CONTENTS

✦

LIST OF FIGURES

✦

MAPS

1
INTRODUCTION

Once upon a time there was a book.

At first, when it appeared on the scene in 1997, *Harry Potter and the Philosopher's Stone* actually was just another book. It's kind of hard to imagine that now, but back then the closest thing I knew of was a picture book for children called *Harvey Potter's Balloon Farm*, which I had read and liked and told my librarian friends so; they'd been eagerly suggesting to me that I read this new book, you see, and I was trying to explain that I *had* read it and stop pestering me.

As it turned out, they weren't talking about a balloon farm at all. They were talking about a wondrous magical world of wizards and witches and enchanted steam trains, a book full of humour and layers of double meanings and hints to a larger mystery. When I did finally read the first Harry Potter book, I wasn't more than five chapters in when I knew that I was hooked. Seriously hooked.

The world of Harry Potter was exactly the kind of world that has always captivated me. I reacted to Harry Potter the way I always do when I encounter a richly detailed and imagined fantasy world. I wanted to list the spells and figure out where the spell words came from (Latin, mostly, I realised, having spent more years than I cared to remember in Latin classes back in high school and college). I wanted to draw maps and collect the interesting and clever new terms like 'Muggle' and 'Diagon Alley'. I wanted to understand it all and catalogue every detail.

I didn't catalogue anything, though. I just read the book. Three times. And waited patiently for the next volume, which had already come out in Britain.

Two things kept me from cataloguing anything, tempting though it was. First of all, I knew how much work it takes to catalogue a world as richly imagined as the one in that Harry Potter book. I'd been cataloguing things like that since I was twelve and taking notes on Star Trek episodes. I love keeping track of all the little details and finding all the connections between things. I particularly enjoy figuring out the background behind those details, such as the sources for story ideas or the etymologies of invented words. But I didn't have time for another hobby, I told myself, and especially one which I knew would take up way too much of my time. The second reason I didn't write things down was more basic. I had heard a few things about the next book, even seen the British cover, and from what I could tell, it had a flying car in it. I didn't think that flying cars fit into the world that had so interested me in the first book, a world of Victorian-era magical alleys crammed with owls and wands and flying broomsticks. I was quite sure that when I read the second book, I wouldn't be particularly excited about Harry Potter after all.

How very wrong I was.

I started reading the second book, *Harry Potter and the Chamber of Secrets*, and made it to page 34 before I gave in to temptation: I grabbed a notebook and started taking notes. The cookbooks in Molly Weasley's kitchen were simply too delicious to ignore, and the mention of 'Celestina Warbeck, the Singing Sorceress' coming from the Wizard Wireless Network radio set was irresistible. I forced myself to stop right where I was, go back to the beginning of the book, and start writing things down. When I finished taking down all the lovely tidbits of information from book two, I went back and took notes on the first book as well. I was off and running.

As more books came along and as I filled my notebooks, I found myself intrigued by the connections between Rowling's invented magical world and the real Britain in which it was set. I have always been an Anglophile, starting as a child with reading *The Secret Garden*, *Winnie the Pooh*, and *Peter Pan*. I loved *Monty Python's Flying Circus* and *Fawlty Towers* back in the 1970s and eagerly read all of James Herriot's books. I read Dickens and Tolkien and C.S. Lewis. I devoured Sherlock Holmes and studied the notes and maps in William S. Baring-Gould's massive *Annotated Sherlock Holmes* (which provided the inspiration for my own Harry Potter reader's guides years later). I studied Shakespeare and the history of Great Britain in college, and discovered one of my favourite books, Josephine Tey's *The Daughter of Time*, in an English literature class with a professor who wore a tweed jacket and smoked a pipe and could have easily passed for the enigmatic Professor Kirke of the Narnia tales.

I realised as I read the Harry Potter stories that although they took place in magical locations, hidden away from non-magical eyes, they were rooted in the very real landscapes and cities of Britain. From the clues in the books, it was possible to place Hogwarts in the Highlands of Scotland. Diagon Alley was just off Charing Cross Road in London. Quidditch was played in remote stadiums on the moors of Cornwall, Devon, and Yorkshire. When I noticed in particular that a number of the names and places were borrowed from the countryside around Exeter where Rowling attended university, I realised that she wrote her books with real places in mind.

My notebooks full of details and descriptions evolved into The Harry Potter Lexicon website, which went live in 2000. As I expanded the website to include more and more background information, I started creating maps of Britain pinpointing some of the more obvious locations from the books, places like Charing Cross Road and Ottery St Mary. Other fans started to get into the game, sending emails with suggestions and writing essays about places in Britain. When one fan sent me an email pinpointing a possible location for Hogwarts castle in Scotland, the idea for this book was born. What would it be like to actually go to some of these places? What would I find there? I wanted to find out. I wanted to explore Britain in search of Harry Potter. In order to do this, I needed clues. I started with the books themselves. When you're a fan of something like Harry Potter, you treat the source material like some sort of mystical gift from the gods. Okay, maybe not quite that, but you get the idea. To fans, every word is important, every concept worthy of dissection, fervent writing, or a six-hour online chat with twelve other fans. Harry

MAGICAL CREATURES IN BRITAIN

Many magical creatures are known to live in Harry Potter's Britain. Some are native to specific regions; others are found throughout the country or all over the world. A lot more information about all the magical creatures noted in this book is available in the book *Fantastic Beasts and Where to Find Them*, which J.K. Rowling wrote for charity.

Some of the most interesting magical creatures of Britain are listed below:

Aethonan This winged 'chestnut' horse is native to Britain. Any wizard who owns one has to place charms on it to hide its wings from Muggles.

Augurey The Augurey is a magical bird with a mournful cry which foretells rain.

Doxy This tiny black flying creature has a nasty bite.

Dugbog Rather like a magical crocodile, this creature looks like a floating log until it bites you in the ankle.

Glumbumble The Glumbumble is a 'grey, furry insect' which causes 'melancholy'.

Graphorn These massive four-legged creatures are purplish, horned, and sometimes ridden by mountain trolls.

Horklump This odd creature is somewhat like a very aggressive mushroom. It's a favourite food of gnomes.

Imp Imps are tiny, mischievous creatures similar to pixies but not able to fly.

Jarvey Resembling a talking overgrown ferret, the Jarvey is fond of insults and rude remarks. It has been known to startle Muggles in their gardens.

Kneazle This magical creature looks like a cat. It is very intelligent and devoted to its witch or wizard master. Crookshanks, Hermione's pet cat, is part Kneazle.

Moke A lizard which can change its size at will in order to hide. Hagrid gives Harry a magical pouch made of Mokeskin for his sixteenth birthday.

Niffler These creatures are cuddly-looking but aggressive when it comes to finding bits of treasure.

Nogtail Although it looks like a small pig, the Nogtail is really a Dark creature which brings 'blight' to a farm where it makes its home.

Troll There are three kinds of troll – mountain, forest and river – but all three are large, stupid, smelly and aggressive, and not the kind of creature one wants around. Harry and Ron once knocked one out with its own club.

SOURCE: *Fantastic Beasts and Where to Find Them* and the novels

Potter devotees aren't the first to dig into a work of fiction this way. Over the years, Sherlock Holmes fans have done the same, working out the location of the detective's Baker Street home and mapping his exploits all over London. Just for the fun of it, they overlook the fact that Holmes and Watson never really lived and charge ahead as if every word of Arthur Conan Doyle's stories is true.

I decided to do the same. I would dive into the text and let myself believe that J.K. Rowling was actually describing real places. I would treat every detail in the books as a possible clue to where these places might be found, then go exploring and try to find them.

Right off the bat, I decided not to go looking for the locations where they filmed the Harry Potter movies. Filmmakers choose their locations based on what will look good on screen; if the locations they choose don't match those in the books, well, so be it. The places shown in the films are wonderful, even magical, but for the most part they don't match the 'real' locations in the books themselves.

I didn't really care to wander aimlessly around Britain, though, hoping to find these magical locations. Britain is a big place. To do the thing properly, I needed time. I moved into a flat near King's Cross Station in London and started planning my adventures.

One of the best sources for information about the world of Harry Potter is my own website, the Harry Potter Lexicon. The information on the site is strictly from the books (well, almost strictly) and all the details are nicely collected by the Lexicon editors and easy to access. Along with the books, I searched the Lexicon for all of the magical places I hoped to visit, beginning with places in and around London itself: Little Whinging, the Ministry of Magic, the Leaky Cauldron, Diagon Alley, St Mungo's Hospital, and Grimmauld Place, noting the clues and details listed there. I also read the essays on the Lexicon written by fans who had a lot of background knowledge about Britain, and chatted with other fans who were willing to point me toward good places to look. Between the Lexicon, friends, and the books, my plans took shape.

One thing I realised as I started planning was that the stories aren't really scattered around Britain as much as I thought. With a few exceptions, almost every event takes place in one of three areas of the country: the area around London; Scotland, where Hogwarts is located; and the West Country, particularly Devon. That made my trips a bit easier to plan.

So off I went, travelling around Britain by foot, bus, train, boat, and car, to find Harry Potter's Britain. I took along a camera, a detailed atlas of Britain, and a GPS device (which turned out to be worth many times its weight in gold Galleons!). I was astonished to discover just how close I could come to visiting Rowling's invented world.

Sources of information: The Harry Potter Series

The Harry Potter novels by J.K. Rowling are the primary source of information about Harry's world. The first book, *Harry Potter and the Philosopher's Stone*, was published in 1997 in Britain and 1998 in the United States, where it was given the title *Harry Potter and the Sorcerer's Stone*.

In this book, I use abbreviations for each book followed by the chapter number to show where I got some bit of information. The abbreviations are listed after each title here.

The Harry Potter series:
Harry Potter and the Philosopher's Stone (1997) (PS)
Harry Potter and the Chamber of Secrets (1998) (CS)
Harry Potter and the Prisoner of Azkaban (1999) (PA)
Harry Potter and the Goblet of Fire (2000) (GF)
Harry Potter and the Order of the Phoenix (2003) (OP)
Harry Potter and the Half-Blood Prince (2005) (HBP)
Harry Potter and the Deathly Hallows (2007) (DH)

In addition to the novels, in 2001 Rowling published two small paperback books which she wrote for charity. These books, which have come to be called the "schoolbooks", provide a wealth of detail about the history and some of magical creatures of the wizarding world of Harry Potter.

The Schoolbooks:
Quidditch Through the Ages (2001) (QA)
Fantastic Beasts and Where to Find Them (2001) (FB)

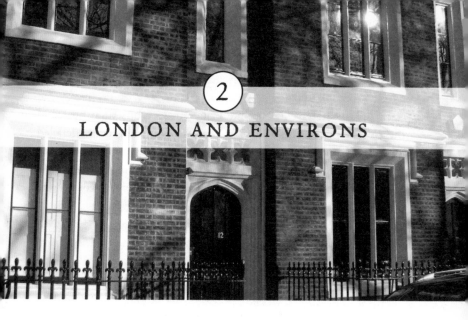

2

LONDON AND ENVIRONS

Since my home base for this whole project was in London, I decided to start my adventures by exploring the city and the surrounding area. More importantly, these are the first places we visit in the books, so it made sense to begin there. Walking the streets of London is quite an experience for an American used to the small towns of the Midwest of the United States. English may be the official voice of the city, politely telling me to 'mind the gap' when exiting a train, but it's far from the only voice I hear: riding the bus or walking down the street, I'm surrounded by conversations in many different accents and languages, only some of which I recognise. People come from all over the world to live and play and set up shop in London. It's possible to find any type of food being served somewhere in London, from French crêpes to Indian chicken tikka masala (which by most accounts was actually invented in Glasgow or Birmingham). From what I tell there are more kebab shops than burger places, and more Starbucks coffee shops than anything else. For a visitor from the Midwest of the United States, London is a dazzling explosion of different cultures, widely varying architecture, and fascinating history.

The buildings of London are an intriguing example of this. They mostly date no farther back than the Great Fire in 1666, for obvious reasons, but the city was actually founded by the Romans two thousand years ago, and bits of their original walls are still visible here and there. As I spent time learning about London, I started to realise that nearly every street and building had some interesting story behind it. The dates carved into many façades indicate that they were built before my home town in the States was anything more than a few shacks along a river in the forest.

And it isn't only the buildings that have tales to tell. Rivers that used to flow through the city have now vanished from view to run underground, popping up above ground every so often as a canal or a pond in a park. Some streets are permanent open-air markets, filled with interesting cooking smells and stalls selling everything from fresh vegetables to cell phone accessories. I had a feeling I was going to find plenty to enjoy in London even if I wasn't a wizard.

Before I started searching in earnest, I did some preliminary exploring, spending some time just wandering through interesting parts of town, getting a feel for the place. Walking through Covent Garden one evening, I felt like I was stepping back in time a hundred years. I'd never been to a city with such an amazing variety of architecture and history. I remarked to my friends that it almost looked like Disneyworld to me, except that this was real. They weren't particularly impressed by this observation and pointed out that no, some parts of Disneyworld just look sort of like London, only without people in costumes. Privately I didn't agree with that last bit. I'd seen some folks in really amazing costumes near some of the clubs. Those were costumes, right?

Once my plans were in place, I was ready to set out. I had gathered my clues and studied the maps. I had an *A–Z*, the ubiquitous street guide to London that is the salvation of tourists and native Londoners alike, and an Oyster card, which would get me onto the buses and the Underground. I was ready to find Harry Potter's London.

First, though, I decided to travel a bit outside of the city, into Surrey. This county to the south-west of London is a mix of rural and suburban areas; the further out you go, though, the less urban the landscape, and not far from central London you're looking at fields and trees and rolling hills. I was excited to ramble through Surrey, as a nice prelude to my city wanderings, and to start my adventure in the same place Rowling started hers.

✦ Little Whinging ✦

In the very first chapter of the first book, we are introduced to one-year-old Harry Potter. This little boy is to become a very remarkable wizard, but we meet him for the first time in a most un-magical place. After the disastrous attack on his family on the evening of October 31 1991 in the West Country village of Godric's Hollow, Harry was rescued by Hagrid, a huge half-giant, and brought on a flying motorcycle to Surrey. Here, in an unremarkable town called Little Whinging, at Number Four Privet Drive, he was left on the doorstep of his only living relative, his mother's Muggle sister Petunia.

Aunt Petunia is married to Vernon Dursley, a large unpleasant fellow who for the next ten years treats Harry very poorly. Vernon is about as much a Muggle as it is possible to be. He doesn't approve of imagination and raises his son, Dudley, to be as boorish and selfish as he is. Vernon intends to squash the magic out of Harry, but fails, of course, and Harry learns at age eleven that he is in fact a wizard and heads off to Hogwarts School of Witchcraft and Wizardry.

The books do give quite a few clues about Little Whinging, so I opened my detailed road atlas of Britain and started looking over the maps of Surrey. I quickly realised that this wasn't going to be easy. At first it seemed like the town could be just about anywhere, and Surrey is a pretty big county.

The house we see in the films, No. 12 Picket Post Close in Bracknell, Berkshire, was built in 1993 along with its identical neighbours. Allegedly chosen as a location precisely because of its lack of distinctive characteristics, the monotonous street is a sort of visual shorthand to signify how boring and mundane Little Whinging is. However, the book description of the house suggests that it is rather older than the one we see in the films. One unusual feature is the chimney – or chimneys, to be accurate. The Dursleys' house has several fireplaces: we learn from the first book that there's one in the living room, but also in that book, and later in book five, we discover that there's another fireplace in the kitchen. This struck me as very unusual. What kind of house has a fireplace in the kitchen? Most likely one which uses the fireplace as a source of heat. Houses built after World War Two in Britain would almost certainly have central heating and fitted kitchens, with gas or electric ovens, rather than stoves requiring chimneys, so fireplaces in those more modern houses would simply be decorative features to be found only in the living room – indeed, for the films chimneys were stuck on to the roofs of the houses in Picket Post Close. The Dursley house must be a bit older, then, maybe built in the 1930s.

FIGURE I
*A house with
pebble-dashed walls*

Another detail supports the idea that the houses in Privet Drive are of a somewhat older style. At least one of the houses nearby is described as having 'pebble-dashed' walls. Houses built after the War might have pebble-dashed walls, but this kind of decoration died out in the 70s, thankfully. Houses in the kind of modern development we see in the films wouldn't be likely to have pebble-dashed walls. Even if the walls and the chimneys suggest an older style, the neighbourhood around Privet Drive is fairly affluent. The houses, which are described in the books as being large and square, have hedges around the gardens and lawns and greenhouses round the back. So the house I want to find won't be in a modern housing estate but in a somewhat older neighbourhood with a variety of styles.

But that isn't enough to tell much about the location: there are probably hundreds of neighbourhoods in Surrey that could fit the description. How could I narrow it down to a particular area?

Two more clues from the books helped me figure out where to look for a neighbourhood like the one described. Unfortunately, these two clues each pointed to a different location.

One clue is the train station Harry uses to get to Little Whinging. In the first book, after Harry learns that he's a wizard, he accompanies Hagrid into London for a day. On the way back to the Dursleys, he and Hagrid travel from Paddington Station. This choice of station seems very odd, since trains from Paddington don't go to Surrey at all. The closest they come is an area of Berkshire just north of Surrey, west of Heathrow Airport. Well, maybe Rowling just made a mistake, you might say. But where's the fun in that? We're going to take her at her word and tease a clue out of it. After all, the book doesn't say that the *station* is in Surrey, just that Little Whinging is. So if Harry got off at the nearest station to Surrey on the train out of Paddington, could he walk or take a bus south to get to Privet Drive, just over the boundary line into Surrey?

As it turns out, this boundary line business gets a bit tricky. The boundaries between Surrey and Berkshire have changed over the past fifteen years and it's hard to know just where the line was in 1991. Little Whinging would have to be pretty close to that ambiguous border to make it worth taking the train from Paddington instead of a train to northern Surrey from Waterloo.

Taking the clues in the book at face value, then, we'll assume that Harry got off the train at Langley or Iver, just north of Surrey in Berkshire. That will give us one possible location for Little Whinging: we'll search to the south of Langley toward Staines, which is in Surrey, and try to find a nice neighbourhood of houses built about seventy years ago with multiple chimneys, hedges, garden walls, greenhouses and lawns.

The second essential clue supports the idea that Little Whinging is located in the northern part of Surrey, to the west of London, but points to a location quite a bit further away than the area near Heathrow. At the beginning of the fifth book, Harry and Dudley are attacked by Dementors in Little Whinging; some time later, members of the Order of the Phoenix arrive to take Harry to their headquarters, located in London at Number 12 Grimmauld Place near King's Cross. They travel from Little Whinging to London on brooms and it takes quite a while to get there – Harry thinks to himself that it feels like an hour. According to Mad-Eye Moody, who is leading the group, they are travelling east almost the whole time, which fits the previous clue.

Interestingly, however, Harry doesn't see the lights of London until near the end of the flight. If Little Whinging were located just to the west of Heathrow Airport, perhaps between Staines and Langley as I've speculated above, the lights of London would have been visible

Number 4 Privet Drive, Little Whinging

Location: Somewhere in Surrey, a county to the south-west of London. The broom flight in book five suggests a location more west than south and in a rural area not too close to London.

Function: The house is the home of the Dursleys: Uncle Vernon, Aunt Petunia, and their son Dudley. As Harry's mother's sister, Petunia Dursley is Harry Potter's only living relative.

How to get there: The house is in the small town of Little Whinging. Most towns in Surrey have train and bus stations. One-year-old Harry arrives there in a slightly more unconventional way, held in the arms of a half-giant riding a flying motorcycle. Since then he has come and gone by car, by broomstick, and by Apparition (disappearing from one place to appear somewhere else). Harry possibly uses a train from Paddington to get there from London, although this is problematic.

Description (outside): The house is neat and tidy and very similar to all the other houses along Privet Drive. In front of the house is a lawn enclosed with a garden wall, a hydrangea bush under the large front window, and a gravel drive. Behind the house is a garden with a greenhouse. Since the house has at least two fireplaces, there will probably be more than one chimney.

Description (inside): The ground floor consists of a kitchen, lounge, dining room and, under the stairs to the upper floor, a cupboard, which Americans would call a closet. The upper floor contains three bedrooms, but Harry didn't get to use one until he was ten years old (Dudley at one time had two bedrooms, to have a place to keep his extra toys). Harry moved into the smallest bedroom, Dudley's objections notwithstanding.

Additional details: Aunt Petunia keeps her house immaculately clean. 'Privet' is a kind of shrub often used as a hedge. There are twelve streetlamps on Privet Drive. The description of the house strongly suggests that it was built no later than the 1930s. There is a playground somewhere nearby, a couple of streets away (OP1).

almost immediately, even with quite a large detour to get around Heathrow Airport and Moody's evasive manoeuvres.

The broom flight suggests, then, a location for Little Whinging quite a bit farther to the west and not too far south. The landscape of Surrey becomes more and more rural the farther we travel from London, which fits with the fact that Harry only sees the lights of London at the end of his journey. Perhaps we'll find Little Whinging around Ascot, Virginia Water, or Camberley.

The trouble is that if Little Whinging was located in those areas, Harry would never have taken a train from Paddington to get there. How can we make sense of that? The essays on the Lexicon website address these questions: Tim Ledbetter, known as the Ravenclaw Rambler, suggests a solution to this problem, pointing out that the book only says that Harry is taking the train from Paddington to get 'back to the Dursleys', not necessarily to their house. Aunt Petunia, Uncle Vernon and Dudley are probably still stranded in the hut on the rock somewhere off the coast, where they'd gone to hide from all the magical letters that had been coming for Harry. Maybe Harry and Hagrid are heading back to that miserable rock in the sea: Paddington Station trains travel toward the West Country and there's plenty of coastline in Devon and Cornwall, or even South Wales, where the rock could be located. So maybe Harry wasn't heading to Surrey at all in book one.

The broom flight in the film

No matter how far west of London Little Whinging is located, it is very unlikely that Harry's broom flight from there to Grimmauld Place would match the one in the film. No reasonable route would take them along the Thames, and certainly not in a westerly direction. For Harry to fly along the particular stretch of the river seen in the film, past the tall office buildings of Canary Wharf and under Blackfriars Bridge, then past the Houses of Parliament, he'd have to be coming in from the other side of the city entirely, and be quite a few miles off course. Perhaps Mad-Eye Moody wanted to do a little sightseeing along the way: Big Ben does look beautiful at night.

FIGURE 2 *A row of houses on a private drive in Camberley*

Anyway, I had two places to look: one rather general, western Surrey towards Camberley; and the other a bit more specific, neighbourhoods between Staines and Langley near Heathrow.

I decided to start my exploration in Camberley, which is just about as far west as you can go and still be in Surrey. I took the train from Waterloo and an hour later found myself on the platform of a small station in the centre of a charming little town. Setting off on foot, I walked down the main street, past the shops, and into a neighbourhood of likely-looking houses. I wandered around looking for hedges and garden walls, but didn't find anything that matched the description in the books until I turned down a private drive. Suddenly I felt like I could be in the right place. The houses were very nice, with lawns and hedges and gravel drives.

I wasn't convinced, however. The street wasn't part of a larger neighbourhood, and, while these houses were quite upscale, those on the surrounding streets weren't. I walked back through the town, this time turning the opposite direction past the station. Once I passed the railway line, I discovered several more likely residential areas. These neighbourhoods had streets that curved and connected

FIGURE 3 *A likely candidate for Number 4 Privet Drive?*

much like those described in the books, and the houses certainly fit the descriptions. I was surprised, however, at just how many trees and hills there were: I had imagined something a bit more flat and uniform and, well, boring. The neighbourhoods I discovered in Camberley were far from boring. They were actually quite beautiful.

The houses weren't particularly new and some had pebble-dashed walls. Although they weren't at all identical, they generally could be described as large and square. I could see hedges and garden walls everywhere. One house in particular struck me as being a perfect match for Number 4. The only thing missing was the gravel drive, although to be fair I didn't sneak into the back garden to see if they had a greenhouse either – I wasn't sure how I would explain myself if the owners caught me at it. I could imagine Uncle Vernon proudly parking his new company car in front of that red garage door, though, and Aunt Petunia peering over the hedges at the neighbours' houses. Now if they only had a hydrangea bush under the front window, I'd have been sold.

Camberley was certainly a good possibility for Little Whinging. As I rode the train back to London, I saw other neighbourhoods around Ascot and Bagshot (another name Rowling borrowed for a character in the books, by the way) that looked a lot like the ones I'd just wandered through. Perhaps the Dursleys' house could be somewhere around there.

But I still had the second possible location to investigate. A few days after my ramble around Camberley, I took the train from Paddington towards Oxford and disembarked at Langley station. Where Camberley had been hilly and looked like a small town, Langley was wide open and flat and felt like suburbia. The fact that jumbo jets were flying over every couple of minutes reminded me that I was still fairly close to the big city. As I walked down the road from the station, I passed an industrial estate; Grunnings, Uncle Vernon's drill company, certainly would have fitted in with the other industries located there.

I walked on past the shops and up the high street, heading south. I had to walk over a mile before I saw the roofs of houses of the type I was seeking. I turned down a small drive with the interesting name of Langley Broom and found a lovely row of houses of the Little Whinging type, but sadly without front gardens or hedges to speak of. These houses looked a lot like the ones in the

FIGURE 4 *Houses near Langley Broom*

film, but as I said, the ones in the film don't match the description of Privet Drive in the books at all, so that wasn't really helpful. Anyway, I had a feeling that staunch Muggle Uncle Vernon would have had a problem living anywhere near a street with the word 'broom' in its name, so I decided I'd have to look further.

Across the road from Langley Broom, I could see the roofs of more houses, some of which seemed to have several chimneys. I walked across the road and down another side street, looking around with interest. I had found my way into a very nice, friendly neighbourhood of older houses. This one even had a playground across the way, as described in book five.

Everywhere I looked here I saw houses that could belong to the Dursleys. Some of the houses had gravel drives. Nearly all had two chimneys. I could see the sunlight glinting on greenhouse roofs in some of the back gardens. I even saw quite a few hydrangea bushes.

I was secretly delighted to notice a van on one street, moving from streetlamp to streetlamp as a worker used a lift to change the bulbs in each one. I remembered that in the first book, Dumbledore used a small device to steal the light from each of the streetlamps on Privet Drive. I was tempted to ask the worker in the van if there

FIGURE 5 *A quiet neighbourhood with large square houses*

FIGURE 6 *My favourite 'Little Whinging' street, this one in Iver*

was some problem with the streetlamps, such as them all going out unexpectedly around midnight, but I thought better of it.

After an hour of wandering, my legs were starting to get sore and I was thinking how comfortable it would be to sit on the train for the trip back to Paddington. I walked back to the station and saw the 12:30 train pulling out, so I knew I'd have a bit of a wait for the next one. I didn't mind, though; I sat on the platform and listened to Stephen Fry read *Half-Blood Prince* on my iPod. When the next train finally came, I climbed aboard and settled down.

But a few minutes later, as the train neared the next stop, I saw another neighbourhood through the window that looked even more like the Privet Drive I imagined. No matter how much my legs were aching and no matter how delightful it was to listen to Fry's interpretation of Narcissa and Bella visiting Snape, I couldn't miss the chance to look around. I hopped off the train at Iver – okay, I didn't exactly hop, but I did manage to drag myself out of my comfortable seat and step wearily onto the platform. The guard told me that there would be another train to Paddington in half an hour, so I set out as quickly as I could.

Once again, I found myself on a lovely street with very nice houses, many with pebble-dashed walls and several chimneys. I had to smile as I walked along the road and noticed neighbours out chatting with each other and parents pushing small children in pushchairs. It occurred to me that my mental picture of Little Whinging had been all wrong. I had been more influenced by the film version than I realised. In fact, the books don't describe a cookie-cutter modern development at all: they describe the kinds of pleasant neighbourhoods I found in Langley and in Camberley.

Then it dawned on me. Little Whinging wasn't boring...the Dursleys were. I don't know if she did it on purpose, but it seemed to me that Rowling was making an interesting point, opposite to the one she made when she chose dreary, mundane locations in London for hiding her magical places. Privet Drive was actually very charming and the houses were interesting and varied: it was the Dursleys themselves who were dreary and mundane. I'll bet the only reason they even had a hydrangea bush at all is because so many of their neighbours did.

I managed to get back to the station in time to catch the next train back to Paddington. As I sank gratefully into my seat and turned my iPod back on, I thought about the fact that I hadn't actually been in Surrey at all that day. Both Langley and Iver are in Berkshire, to the north of Surrey. Neither of those places could be the 'real' Little Whinging, then. However, it was clear that small communities like these are common in this part of the country; and, to be fair, the street in which they filmed the Privet Drive scenes for the first movie wasn't in Surrey either, but in Bracknell, which is also in Berkshire and just a few miles from Langley and Iver. In fact, the movie people have now actually built a set of the Bracknell street at Leavesden Studios in Hertfordshire, which isn't Surrey either.

Oh well. So where is Privet Drive? From what I discovered, just about everywhere. And it's a pretty nice place.

✦ Greater London ✦

On his eleventh birthday, Harry discovers an amazing secret: he learns from Hagrid that he is a wizard and that he has been accepted to study at Hogwarts School of Witchcraft and Wizardry. Hagrid takes him into London to buy all the strange and magical things he'll need for school; this trip, described in the first book, introduces Harry to the magical world of which he's a part. It also introduces him to the city of London, which according to the book he's never visited before that day.

But wait, what about the zoo he visits on Dudley's birthday just a month before? The film shows him visiting the London Zoo in Regent's Park. But the book makes it clear that he had never been to London before when he goes there with Hagrid, so this can't be

MAGICAL CREATURES IN LONDON

While the busy streets of London seem an unlikely place to find magical creatures, some interesting beasts do make their home in (or beneath) the city.

Crup This magical dog 'resembles a Jack Russell terrier', and if it weren't for the forked tail, you might not be able to tell one from the other. In fact, witches and wizards who raise Crups are required to remove the tale (painlessly by magic) to keep their magical nature a secret. Crups were originally bred in this area of Britain.

Sphinx This mysterious creature originated in Egypt, but Gringotts has imported a few of them to guard underground vaults. The sphinx asks a person a riddle before letting them pass, which some vault owners find a bit annoying. (DP1)

Dragon As unlikely as it seems, a few dragons live far below the streets of London, brought in by the Goblins to protect the high security bank vaults. These dragons are terribly abused and live their long lives chained in the darkness.

Pigeon Well, okay, no, pigeons aren't in the least bit magical. Sorry.

SOURCES: *Fantastic Beasts and Where to Find Them*, the Daily Prophet newsletters, and the novels

the zoo he went to with the Dursleys. Maybe Harry didn't think of the zoo visit as a trip to London because Regent's Park isn't *central* London. But if he actually hadn't been to London before his eleventh birthday, what other zoo could it be?

Unfortunately, there aren't a lot of other possibilities anywhere near Little Whinging, whichever part of Surrey we choose to put it in. The zoo described in the book has a reptile house, which is fairly common in zoos, but it also has gorillas. Only the large zoos have gorillas. There is a zoo called Chessington in Surrey with both a reptile house and gorillas, which would fit the bill quite nicely. It doesn't seem to have a boa constrictor in its reptile house, according to the website, but that's okay – we Harry Potter fans remember that the zoo's boa constrictor escaped in 1991, after all. However, Chessington is part of a larger theme park called Chessington World of Adventures. According to the book, Dudley gets very bored with looking at the animals by lunchtime; surely he would have demanded to go on the theme park rides long before then, and just as surely his parents would have let him. However, Chessington is probably the most likely zoo that they would have visited in the area of Little Whinging. As for Dudley not going on the rides all morning, perhaps Uncle Vernon and Aunt Petunia insisted that he spend some time seeing the animals first because it was educational? Unlikely.

At any rate, a month later Harry visits London with Hagrid and finds his way to some amazing and surprising magical places. I was eager to do the same.

London is definitely a place of surprises. Next to a modern office tower on a busy street you might find an ancient pub, an ornate church, or something that resembles a medieval castle. The streets curve and intersect at odd angles and change names without warning. Every now and then you find a unique shop, like the one on New Oxford Street that sells only umbrellas and walking sticks.

Each time Harry visits London, he finds a magical place hidden away somewhere behind or beneath this higgledy-piggledy city landscape. When he comes to London in book one, clutching his shopping list, Hagrid tells him that he can buy everything he needs in London if he knows where to look. Sure enough, in the midst of a busy Muggle street, Harry discovers a tiny pub called the Leaky

Cauldron and behind that a magical doorway which leads into Diagon Alley, a secret High Street filled with shops that sell every sort of magical item a witch or wizard could want.

A month later, Harry is back in London. This time he discovers a hidden gateway in King's Cross railway station to Platform Nine and Three-Quarters, where he boards the Hogwarts Express for his journey to Hogwarts School of Witchcraft and Wizardry.

On a later trip to London, Harry finds the house of his godfather, Sirius Black, in an unassuming square called Grimmauld Place. From there he is escorted to the Ministry of Magic, a vast underground complex from which the wizarding world is governed, and to St Mungo's Hospital for Magical Maladies and Injuries, which is disguised as an abandoned department store. Each of these magical places is cleverly hidden away in the bustling Muggle city. London is simply bursting with magical buildings and streets in the stories. I was off to find them.

PLACES TO FIND

London

King's Cross Station: location of Platform Nine and Three-Quarters, where witches and wizards board the Hogwarts Express train

Grimmauld Place: a run-down square near King's Cross where the Black family home is located, hidden behind enchantments

Charing Cross Road: location of The Leaky Cauldron, a small 'grubby-looking pub' with a magical doorway at the back into Diagon Alley

St Mungo's Hospital for Magical Maladies and Injuries: hidden away behind the façade of an abandoned department store

The Ministry of Magic: located underground, reached via a telephone box on a side street in the heart of London

✦ Platform Nine and Three-Quarters ✦

King's Cross Station was an obvious place to start my explorations of London. For one thing, it's easy to find, even for an American like myself who gets lost easily: I just walked down the street from my flat and followed the signs and the steady stream of people walking in that direction, pulling their luggage. I had a feeling that the other places I hoped to find wouldn't be quite so well marked.

King's Cross plays a key role in the stories right from the beginning. In the first book, poor Harry finds himself alone in the station without anyone to show him how to get to the platform he needs in order to catch the Hogwarts Express at eleven o'clock. He asks a guard to direct him to 'Platform Nine and Three-Quarters', but the man ridicules him. He's about to despair when he overhears a family of red-headed kids and their mother mention the word 'Muggles'

FIGURE 7 *King's Cross Station*

Platform Nine and Three-Quarters

Location: King's Cross Station, which is on Euston Road in the north part of central London, next to St Pancras International Station and half a mile down the road from Euston Station.

Function: Railway platform where witches and wizards board the Hogwarts Express.

How to get there: Walk through the metal barrier between platforms nine and ten at King's Cross Station. Mrs Weasley suggests doing it at a "bit of a run" (PS6).

Description (King's Cross side): The barrier between platforms nine and ten which Harry walks through is metal and there is a ticket box there (Harry wonders whether he's supposed to tap it with his wand to get through) (PS6). The area around the entrance is busy, with crowds of people passing by.

Description (Magical platform): Through the magical entrance, a stream train waits at an old-fashioned railway platform. A wrought-iron sign saying 'Platform Nine and Three-Quarters' hangs over the exit back to Muggle King's Cross (PS6), at which a guard monitors how many people go back at the same time through the gate into King's Cross itself, since too many people appearing out of nowhere could be noticed by the Muggles passing by on the other side (PS17).

Additional details: As the Hogwarts Express pulls out of the station, it rounds a bend (PS6). Mr Weasley parks his Ford Anglia on a side road near King's Cross (CS5). The platform has to be quite long, since the Hogwarts Express has enough carriages to hold over three hundred pupils. According to legend, Boudica, the warrior queen of the Britons who fought the Romans in AD 60 or 61, died in battle in the area which is now King's Cross and was buried under platforms 9 and 10.

and realises that they must be going to the same place he is. With their help, he finds the magical portal hidden behind a metal barrier between platforms nine and ten. I couldn't expect to get help from a family of wizards in King's Cross so I had to do the best I could on my own. But how hard could it be to find a couple of railway platforms, I asked myself?

I walked down the street and saw the huge and ornate St Pancras station in the distance. I didn't notice until I was quite close to it, but there, right next door, is King's Cross. The station's Victorian archways and towers might have been beautiful once, but now they're hidden behind a hulking covered extension over the pavement, painted the standard railway station green. This monstrosity, built in 1972, was supposed to be temporary, but sadly it's still there. There are plans to remove it and create an open plaza, which would be a welcome change.

I almost felt sorry for King's Cross, squatting there like a toad next to St Pancras, whose glorious red brick Gothic architecture draws everyone's eye. Personally, if I was going to choose a station to be a

FIGURE 8 *King's Cross interior*

magical waypoint, I would have gone with St Pancras. They did do that in the film, by the way – when Ron flies his father's car up into the sky to follow the Hogwarts Express in the second movie, he's flying past St Pancras, not King's Cross. It's a lot prettier, after all, and a lot more magical. As a matter of fact, if you want to take a train to a magical place, catching the Eurostar from St Pancras direct to Disneyland Paris is about as close as you could hope to come.

But King's Cross was my destination today. I walked through the milling crowds coming up out of the Underground station and through the automatic glass doors into King's Cross itself.

The interior of King's Cross, if anything, is even more boring than the outside. I couldn't help but notice just how ordinary the station was; it's merely a waypoint, a place through which people walk quickly with their thoughts on their final destination. Some people walk through reading a book or newspaper without even glancing around them. Many are firmly hidden in their private world, listening to music only they can hear through their iPod earphones. Everything is metal and plastic. Metal barriers and cold plastic signs lead passengers past small coffee shops and kiosks and point the way to the platforms beyond. The trains are long, smooth, growling metal

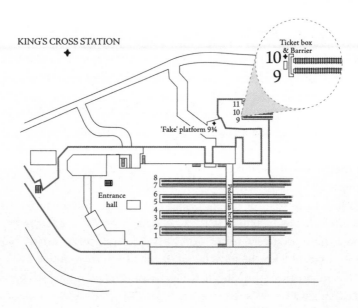

things with no hint of romance or excitement. The only fauna visible are the pigeons prospecting for scraps of food.

In short, King's Cross is a very unlikely place to find anything at all magical. I'm sure that Rowling did this on purpose, contrasting the modern, sterile King's Cross to the enchanted world Harry discovers on the other side of the barrier between platforms nine and ten. On the magical platform he sees not a modern diesel train but a puffing bright red steam engine. Instead of hiding behind their earphones or copies of the day's newspaper, the passengers chat excitedly, carrying owls and school trunks, calling out to friends and hugging their families. Cats wend their way between the legs of the people on the platform. One student even shows off a large spider in a box to his friends. The gate over the entrance is not modern plastic but Victorian wrought iron. The smoky, steamy air is filled with a sense of wonder and magic. The boring Muggle world of King's Cross station is nowhere to be seen.

Harry travels through King's Cross many times in the books, on his way to or from Hogwarts School of Witchcraft and Wizardry. In the last book, however, he visualises the station in a very different way. In the midst of his climactic confrontation with the evil Lord Voldemort, Harry imagines himself in King's Cross again, but this time the station is a waypoint between life and death, where he meets Dumbledore, his mentor. This 'dream' King's Cross is white and airy, with no other people around at all. Harry senses that he is in a station, in that he is in a temporary place between moving on to somewhere far away or returning to the life he has just left. In this vision, Dumbledore gently tells him that if he so chooses, he can simply 'board a train' to go on to the afterlife. He sits with his old Headmaster and ponders which direction to go, gazing up at the arched glass roof far overhead. In this scene, King's Cross is otherworldly, even sacred.

Once I was past the monitors and had walked onto the platforms themselves, I looked up at that vast glass and steel roof and thought about how strangely fitting this location was for Harry's final confrontation with the meaning of his life. Even surrounded by the noise and bustle of the Muggle King's Cross, I found myself strangely awed. In a way, it resembles a cathedral, although the glass is stained

FIGURE 9 *King's Cross roof*

with grime and age, not colours. I wonder how many people who trudge through the station ever look up at that vast glass and steel roof and notice how beautiful it really is.

After a few moments looking up, lost in thoughts of cathedrals and stained glass, I remembered what I was looking for and moved along, with pigeons fluttering out of my path. I wandered around the station trying to spot platforms nine and ten. At first I thought there weren't that many platforms, since the numbers on the signs by the tracks in the main station only go up to eight. Clearly, if they existed at all, these platforms weren't located in the main part of the station under the arched roof.

Finally I saw a sign pointing out the additional platforms and followed it down the length of platform eight, past the crossover bridge that is featured in the films. As I walked along, the train to my right growled into life and started moving off towards daylight. Watching its progress out of the far end of the train shed, I realised that there was a problem. Not with the train – it rumbled away just fine – but in the description of King's Cross in the books. The Hogwarts Express is described as rounding a curve as it leaves the station. But trains leaving King's Cross don't go around a curve at all; instead they disappear into one of two large tunnels. How was I going to explain that?

After the train was gone, I took my bearings again and followed another sign down a narrow passage leading off to the left. I came face to face with two guards, neither of whom looked like they'd care about something as fanciful as a magical doorway. They asked for my ticket. Rather sheepishly, I told them I was looking for Platform Nine and Three-Quarters, keenly aware of the fact that I was likely to get the same brush-off that Harry got when he asked that question in book one. To my surprise, however, the guards nodded and pointed around to the left.

I looked where they indicated and saw, next to the passageway to platforms nine, ten, and eleven, a walkway leading to the street where the taxis waited, towards St Pancras Station next door. I left the guards to take tickets from genuine passengers and I walked down the passageway, feeling a bit foolish. But the guards were right. There along the walkway was a wall with a brick arch, over which was a sign reading 'Platform 9¾'. A luggage trolley was sticking out of the wall. Not really sticking out of the wall, of course – the folks running the station had chopped a trolley in half and fastened it to the bricks for the benefit of tourists like me. Passers-by looked on bemusedly as I pushed on the wall and jiggled the luggage trolley. Needless to say, the wall remained solid. Jaded Londoners barely looked up, but no sooner had I walked away from the wall than another group of people walked up, jiggled the trolley with huge smiles on their faces, and took pictures of each other under the sign. Tourists and fans, just like me. I wondered how many of those Londoners pointedly looking away had actually walked up and pushed on that cart at some point, just like I did.

FIGURE 10 *Platform Nine and Three-Quarters, next to the passage to platforms 9, 10, and 11*

FIGURE 11
The 'official' Platform Nine and Three-Quarters at King's Cross

The wall and the luggage trolley were fun, but they didn't match the description in the books at all. The barrier described in the books is metal, not brick, and seems to be located in a fairly busy part of the station: Harry's view of the barrier is obscured by groups of people walking by. It's clearly supposed to be between two platforms. None of this was true of the brick archway I was looking at. Oh, it would be pretty easy for a group of witches and wizards to sidle down this passageway between stations and to disappear through this brick wall without drawing undue attention to themselves, as long as the tourists weren't standing there having their pictures taken. But it was clear that this wall was chosen because it vaguely resembles the gateway in the films, not the one in the books.

I walked back to the guards and asked if I could just pop through to get a few pictures of platforms nine and ten. I had the distinct impression that I wasn't the first person to ask this question. They let me past.

There they were. Platforms nine and ten at King's Cross. Harry had looked at those same plastic numbers and wondered how to find his way into the magical world. I tried to imagine him standing

FIGURE 12 *Platforms Nine and Ten at King's Cross, with a ticket machine between them*

right here where I was, wondering what to do. In front of me was a metal railing and above it a row of monitors announcing the next trains. A ticket machine and a row of advertising posters filled up the space between the platforms. The ticket machine was a good sign – Harry wonders in the book if he shouldn't tap the ticket box between platforms nine and ten to get through.

I glanced around. Behind me were turnstiles leading out into the street and several more guards. There really wasn't a lot of space for groups of people to walk past and obscure Harry's view, and since the platforms were in a separate building off to the side, they weren't exactly crowded. But I wasn't going to be deterred. This was the actual place, after all: between platforms nine and ten at King's Cross Station. I pushed against the metal pillar to the right of the ticket machine that held up the row of monitors overhead. Nothing, of course. I couldn't easily reach the metal barrier itself. I stepped back and surveyed the area. The platforms here were much shorter than the ones in the main train shed; I wondered if a train with six carriages would even fit. Beyond, the tracks disappeared into the same tunnels I'd seen in the main terminal. No curve. Still, it was fun to imagine Harry and the Weasleys, laden with trunks and owls and who knows what, slipping through that metal pillar there, just to the right of the ticket machine.

I walked back out into the sunshine. I had read an interview in which Rowling had explained that the scene of Harry's first visit to Platform Nine and Three-Quarters had come to her while she was on a train in Manchester, adding that she had mistakenly been visualising the platforms at Euston Station when she described the metal barrier which the Weasleys and Harry go through. Euston Station is just down Euston Road from King's Cross and St Pancras; I wondered if I might find a more appropriate location there, so I set off down the street to see what she had had in mind.

Along the way, I looked around for a place where Mr Weasley could have parked his Ford Anglia. In the film, the car is parked right in front of St Pancras, in a bus and taxi space and blocking a walkway, attracting glares from passers-by. That's not in the books, though, which say Harry and Ron come back out of King's Cross and find the car parked down a side street. I glanced up and down the roads

FIGURE 13 *The main entrance to Euston Station*

between the two stations, but there was no parking anywhere, nor along Euston Road. There weren't even any side streets, just busy main roads. I wouldn't be surprised if Mr Weasley did in fact park in a taxi rank or a bus lane, just like they show in the film. I could only guess what consternation that would create.

I almost walked right past Euston Station. It's set quite a distance back from Euston Road behind a blocky modern office building. Even the fact that this building is set on pillars above the bus station isn't enough to make it in the least bit interesting to look at. I had seen pictures of the incredible, seventy-foot-tall marble archway, modelled on the entrance to the Acropolis, which had once stood here as the entrance to the station; how disappointing it must have been when that arch was removed in the 1960s to be replaced with an office building, as plain and boring as all the others around it. The arch now survives only as a mosaic symbol on the wall of the Underground station.

Unlike the arches and towers of King's Cross or the soaring red spires of St Pancras, the façade of Euston Station itself is completely

FIGURE 14
The glorious arch
which used to mark
the entrance to
Euston Station

modern, square and plain. I walked through the doors and found myself in a large concourse with monitors overhead announcing arrivals and departures. It looked a lot like King's Cross.

I couldn't see the trains, though. The platforms, as it turned out, are beyond the entrance hall, down sloping tunnels. I followed the signs to platforms nine and ten, only to discover that here, just like at King's Cross, I would need a ticket to get through. I could see the platforms I wanted just beyond the ticket gates, so I chatted with one of the guards and asked if he might let me step through just for a few minutes to take some pictures. He was quite intrigued by my explanation of taking pictures for a book about Harry Potter, and asked a few questions about why I was at Euston Station instead of King's Cross. Apparently he was a bit of a fan of the books because he let me through. It didn't hurt that I was carrying two cameras, an A–Z, a notebook, and a dog-eared paperback copy of *Harry Potter and the Philosopher's Stone*; I imagine I looked way too geeky to be a terrorist.

Platforms nine and ten at Euston looked pretty similar to those I'd seen at King's Cross. There was a little more space around them, but there were no crowds of people here either to hide someone pushing through a magical barrier. Then again, if a train had just come in, there might be crowds making their way toward the tunnels back to the entrance hall.

Here, as in King's Cross, a metal railing stood between platforms nine and ten. If I walked straight from the tunnel and kept going, I'd smack right into that metal barrier. Unlike King's Cross, however, there was no ticket machine. I looked down the tracks toward the place where the trains would exit the station. There were no tunnels, which was good, but no curves either.

There was quite a bit of room here, though, and I could imagine families of witches and wizards trotting down that sloping tunnel surrounded by commuters and tourists, and simply walking straight through and out of sight. The railway platforms were certainly long enough to handle the Hogwarts Express. The barrier was a lot easier to get to, as well: no monitors, no advertisements, just a nice wide expanse of metal railing.

As I was taking pictures and imagining Harry with his trunk and owl, a different guard strolled over, talking on a mobile phone. While he talked he leaned casually on the barrier between platforms nine and ten, exactly in the middle. He was standing right where the magical gateway would be.

But where would that platform be exactly? Neither the tracks at King's Cross nor at Euston had any space between them. If I could really have walked through the barriers at either station, I would have ended up standing in the three feet of space between two tracks, once I picked myself up from the fall, that is. There is certainly no room for a hidden platform there.

FIGURE 15 *The barrier between platforms nine and ten at Euston*

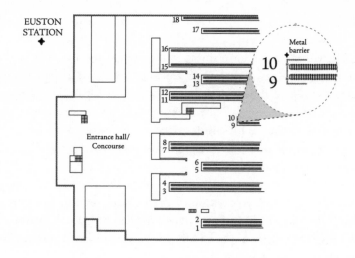

Obviously, Platform Nine and Three-Quarters isn't one of the 'real' platforms or simply invisible. The gateway must lead into some magical space existing out of sight of the Muggles, a platform that gives access to a train on a track that no one can see. I thought about that for a moment. That would mean that the magical platform wouldn't even have to be orientated in the same direction as the platforms in the Muggle station. Perhaps the curve described in the books comes from the train looping around out of the magical space to connect up to the 'real' railway line beyond the station. But how would a scarlet steam train be able to appear on the Muggle tracks out of nowhere? Where would that happen? Then it dawned on me. The tunnels! They would make a perfect place for the Hogwarts Express to pop back into the non-magical world and join the tracks heading north. Hey, I liked that idea.

So which is it, King's Cross or Euston? Either one will do, but despite what Rowling said, I'm going with King's Cross. While there might be more space around the platforms at Euston, there is no ticket box to be seen. That ticket box is so prominent in the books that Harry is afraid he's going to smash into it when he's running toward the barrier. But it's more than that. Let's face it, it's just plain cool to stand in King's Cross looking at platforms nine and ten, and thinking that with a little push just there...

✦ Number 12 Grimmauld Place ✦

My next goal was to find Grimmauld Place. This small, grungy square is the location of the family home of Sirius Black, Harry's godfather. There were innumerable possible candidates in London, but I had a few clues to work with which I hoped would narrow things down quite a bit. One particularly helpful bit of information was the fact that a group of people walk from Number 12 Grimmauld Place to King's Cross Station, carrying all their luggage for the trip to Hogwarts and walking for about twenty minutes to get there. That would put Grimmauld Place about a mile or so from King's Cross. So I needed to find a quiet, run-down square within the area around that station. Piece of cake, I thought.

Finding a quiet spot in London is surprisingly easy. You wouldn't think so wandering down the main streets, since London, like New York or any other large city, is noisy, busy, and filled with people, even late at night. Turn off a main street, however, and you just might end up in a tree-filled square where the sound of traffic is reduced to the occasional passing car and where you can actually hear birds singing and see flowers and trees.

Walking towards Rosebery Avenue from King's Cross, I took a detour down a side street and found just such a square. The houses surrounding it looked a lot like the ones in the film version of Grimmauld Place, and since it's within the correct distance of King's Cross, I was tempted to believe that this square was the location of the Black ancestral home. Trouble was, Grimmauld Place is described as being a small square of unkempt grass surrounded by grimy houses with broken windows and peeling paint, some with heaps of rubbish on their front steps. This square was fairly large and well-tended, and the streets around the square were very clean, as city streets go. I wondered what this square looked like in the 1990s. Has it been 'prettied up' since then?

I tried to imagine that Number Twelve was hidden away somewhere along that square, but I wasn't convinced. This square didn't fit all the clues very well. Even if it were shabbier back in the 1990s, it wasn't in the right place in relation to the Underground

Number 12 Grimmauld Place

Location: On a square within 20 minutes' walk from King's Cross by a group of people laden with luggage, therefore within about a one-mile radius of the station (OP10).

Function: The ancestral home of the Black family, inherited by Harry Potter.

How to get there: The house is magically hidden with a Fidelius Charm, so the only way to see the house at all is to know where it is. For someone who has been given the secret, the house will magically appear by 'pushing aside' the adjacent houses.

Description (from the square): The exterior of the house is old and poorly maintained. There is rubbish on the pavements and by the doors of the other houses. The square is small and unkempt. The knocker on the black front door is in the shape of a serpent and made of silver.

Description (inside): The house has four floors, plus a basement and an attic, which makes it really quite enormous as houses of this kind go. Perhaps the inside of the house is larger than the outside, in typical wizarding fashion. The basement is the kitchen. The ground floor contains the entrance hall, a staircase to the upper floors, and a dining room. The first floor is the drawing room where the Black family tree tapestry hangs. The second floor is where Harry and Ron's bedroom is, and possibly other bedrooms. The third floor contains more bedrooms, including that of Regulus Black. Sirius's room is on the fourth floor, and there is also an attic above this. The house is dank and infested with magical pests and Dark Magic items. Stuffed house-elf heads are mounted on the wall of the stairway.

Additional details: Located a few streets away from a "miserable little Underground station" which is at least four stops away from the "heart of London" (OP7). There is probably a gate opposite number 12, if the square is fenced, which it almost certainly is.

stations mentioned in the books. Tim Ledbetter, who had written several of the excellent essays for the Lexicon under the pseudonym 'Ravenclaw Rambler', worked in London, so I shot him an email and asked for advice.

He met me at King's Cross on a sunny afternoon. Tim is incredibly knowledgeable about London, and he explained to me that by using the descriptions in the books of Underground journeys from Grimmauld Place, he had worked out that the dingy square with the enchanted old house had to be somewhere near Camden Town, Caledonian Road, or Mornington Crescent Tube stations, to the north of King's Cross. Harry and Mr Weasley walk a few streets from Grimmauld Place to get to a 'miserable' station, which is at least four stops from the heart of London. We took the Underground to Camden Town station and set out on foot to see what we could see nearby.

FIGURE 16 *A quiet square near King's Cross*

FIGURE 17 "...saw two houses connected to each other, one house well-kept while the other was falling apart"

I noticed immediately that we were in a more suitable area. The houses were a lot less fancy and many were derelict. More than once I saw two houses connected to each other, one house well-kept while the other was falling apart. Most of these houses were only a few storeys high, but since the house we were looking for is magical, that wouldn't necessarily be a problem. A bigger problem was the fact that there aren't any squares in this part of London. I saw a few scraps of grass with a tree or two, but nothing resembling a square.

We walked around the area looking for likely locations. I did see a small triangle of grass with a few trees across from a row of houses and took a picture. It wasn't an exact match, but I figured it could stand in for Grimmauld Place at a pinch.

Then we headed for Mornington Crescent station. Tim told me that Mornington Crescent would be the best match of the three stations he'd mentioned, but that it had been closed for most of the 1990s for lift repairs. That's the timeframe of the books, unfortunately. Still, I wanted to take a look at the famous Mornington Crescent station, which features prominently in a very strange game on the BBC radio

FIGURE 18 *Houses and a small 'square' (more of a triangle) near King's Cross*

FIGURE 19 *Mornington Crescent station*

comedy show *I'm Sorry I Haven't A Clue*. I have to admit that I have
tried to understand how the game is played and, no, I haven't a clue.
But since I'd seen all the other big sights in London, including Big
Ben and Tower Bridge, I had to see Mornington Crescent as well.

As I said, the station near Grimmauld Place is described as a "miserable little Underground station." Mornington Crescent isn't exactly miserable, but it's small and a bit run down. Tim and I walked around, looking for any houses which could fit. Just two streets over we spotted a very promising row of houses. The numbers even matched, and there was no number 12 immediately visible between numbers 11 and 14. This may have been because numbers 12 and 13 were tucked around the corner on the side street, but still.

I wished I could find a square, though, or even a patch of grass. All these likely houses were on long streets, both here and nearer Camden Town. The fact of the matter is, with no squares to speak of in the area, nowhere that I could find in the correct part of London north of King's Cross would fit the description exactly.

Tim pointed out that Rowling had actually lived a bit north of where we were, in Tufnell Park. It was possible that she was imagining a square that she'd seen when she lived there, but simply underestimated the amount of time it would take to walk to King's Cross. Unfortunately, he said, there weren't really any squares in that area either. We had to admit that we were stymied.

There was plenty of territory still to explore, but Tim had to catch the Tube and go back to work. I thanked him profusely for spending his lunch break wandering around Camden with me and asked if

FIGURE 20 *Near Mornington Crescent. Number 11 is on the end on the right*

he'd mind if I included his essay in this book. He agreed, and you'll find the essay in the Appendix.

Like I said, there was still plenty of ground to cover. After all, Tim and I hadn't checked everywhere. My friend Rachael came to the rescue. She traced a one-mile diameter circle around King's Cross on Google Earth, pinpointed all the Underground stations within that circle, and worked out just as Tim had done which stations would qualify as being run-down and more than four stops from the heart of London. She then proceeded to pore over the *A–Z* looking for anything resembling a square within a few streets of those stations. Just for good measure, she used the Transport for London website to learn how many minutes' walk each of these squares was from King's Cross. The Internet is a wonderful thing.

There weren't very many squares that qualified, as it turned out, and all of them were clustered very close to two stations: Highbury & Islington and Caledonian Road. She circled them on the map and handed it to me. There were seven very likely possibilities. Ah, the thrill of the hunt. I grabbed the camera and we headed out.

FIGURE 21 *A one-mile radius around King's Cross*

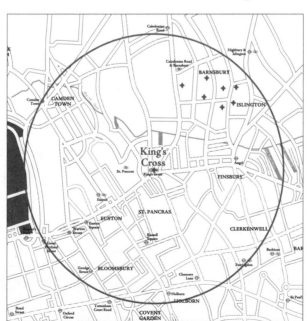

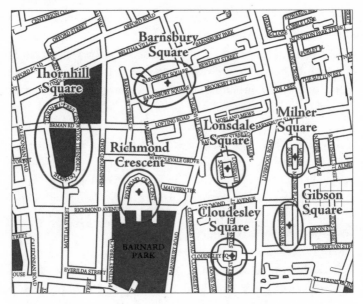

FIGURE 22 *Squares about 20 minutes' walk from King's Cross and near a run-down Tube station which is at least four stops from the heart of London*

One of these squares could be Grimmauld Place, if the clues in the book were correct. We plotted our course, starting with Thornhill Square, just off Caledonian Road and about eighteen minutes' walk from King's Cross.

Thornhill Square wasn't small, it was actually very large. It wasn't unkempt either, but neatly landscaped. The houses bordering it looked a lot like the houses on the square near my flat, not in the least bit run-down. I looked for number 12 and found it. Interestingly, number 11 next door was noticeably shabbier than the houses around it. None of these houses were tall enough to fit the description in the books, though, and that plus the large tidy square convinced me that I had to look further.

As we walked on toward the next possibility, I wondered why the Black family would live in a run-down neighbourhood. It was possible that it had been nicer once but had fallen into disrepair around them while they hid behind their magical defences. It's also possible that the square wasn't really as run-down as Harry thinks, simply because he's used to living in a salubrious neighbourhood in the suburbs

FIGURE 23
Thornhill Square

FIGURE 24
*(below) Number
12 Thornhill Square,
on the right, with the
somewhat shabbier
number 11 next door*

and doesn't realise that cities are typically dirtier and messier places than those he's used to. We're seeing almost the entire story through Harry's eyes, after all.

Either way, the squares I had found in London thus far were all very pleasant places with smart houses around them. We walked on to Barnsbury Square, a little way down the road. While this was marginally less fancy than Thornhill Square, it was essentially the same. The square was almost a well-tended park, and the houses were of the same kind I'd seen before.

Next we walked over to Milner Square and, just beyond that, Gibson Square. I was starting to get a sense of déjà vu. Every one of these squares looked pretty much like the others; I really couldn't choose one over the other as being a better fit. Any one of them would do. I was starting to think that every square in London was identical.

FIGURE 25 *Yet another possibility for Grimmauld Place…*
these squares all started to look alike to me at this point

And then we walked into Lonsdale Square.

I knew immediately that I had finally found Grimmauld Place. This square was different, a surprise. The houses looked nothing like those on the other squares, with their smooth façade and straight roof-line: here they towered four storeys to pitched roofs.

We found number 12 opposite a gate into the small grassy square. That fits the book. And the door to number 12? Black. Seriously. It didn't have a snake door knocker, but it was set back a little in the brick wall. I loved the feel of the place. It was completely unique. Oh, and the walking time to King's Cross was twenty-four minutes.

FIGURE 26
(above)
Lonsdale Square

FIGURE 27
Number 12
Lonsdale Square

All we needed to do now was walk to the nearest Under-ground station and see if it could be described as "miserable". The closest station would be Highbury & Islington, which we could get to by walking down Barnsbury Street to Upper Street and then north to Highbury Corner.

I had taken pictures of several other stations nearby and while they weren't exactly fancy, they were classic Tube stations, built in the early 1900s. The red arched façade of Mornington Crescent, for example, stood at the junction of two busy streets, opposite a statue and next to a park. Caledonian Road was a bit older and dirtier, but it still had the typical cheerful red-tiled arched architecture. I don't think that anyone would call it 'miserable', just somewhat ordinary. We walked along Upper Street towards Highbury & Islington station. I wondered what I'd find.

I almost didn't find it at all. The station was hidden away behind a building. But when I did spot it, I knew I had found the station I wanted. A lot of people were coming and going through what looked like the doors to someone's garage. I tried to hold back a wide smile. I was very likely the only one who was happy to see such an unimpressive, dilapidated station.

FIGURE 28
Typical red arches at
Caledonian Road station

LONDON AND ENVIRONS 49

FIGURE 29   A "miserable little Underground station" near Lonsdale Square

Highbury & Islington Station wasn't always like this. The current building was constructed on the site of a very grand and impressive station which was hit by a V-1 flying bomb during World War Two. A piece of that old building is still visible to the left of the entrance. A more traditional, red-arched station stands across the street, but it was taken out of service when several Underground and aboveground rail services were combined in this current underwhelming building. The London Underground people are well aware that this station is in need of an upgrade and are planning improvements. But for now, it's just plain miserable-looking. And just to be sure, I checked how far it was from the 'heart of London' and discovered that it's four stops on the Victoria Line from Oxford Circus, which is right in the middle of the city. I was thrilled.

After all my hours of wandering around, staying within a twenty-minute walk of King's Cross, I finally felt like we'd found Grimmauld Place, there in Lonsdale Square. I hoped I would be as lucky finding other places in London…and I hoped I wouldn't have to walk quite so far to find them. My feet hurt. We took the bus back to King's Cross.

St Mungo's Hospital for
Magical Maladies and Injuries

St Mungo's magical hospital, my next quarry, was to be found hiding inside a disused department store called Purge and Dowse Ltd, near a Tube station in the heart of London. The store, according to a passing Muggle in book five, has been closed for refurbishment for years. It's built of red brick and has a display window where a dilapidated mannequin stands, sporting out-of-date clothing. If you're magical, you will be greeted by the mannequin and beckoned through the window and into the hospital's reception.

At first, I thought St Mungo's might be as easy to find as King's Cross. There really is a St Mungo's in London, after all: it's a charity organisation which works with homeless people, giving them shelter and helping them get back on their feet. It's named after an actual person, Saint Mungo, who lived in the late sixth century and, amongst other achievements, founded the city of Glasgow. An organisation that helps the homeless is something that Rowling might have known about, even supported. On the other hand, there's a St Mungo's cathedral in Glasgow which Rowling might also have known about, so it could just be a coincidence. Or maybe Rowling chose 'Mungo' simply because it has that slightly odd sound to it that is typical of Wizarding names in her stories. At any rate, I thought that maybe their headquarters would be a red-brick building that has prominent ground floor windows.

I was partly right. The building, I discovered, is in fact made of red brick. I had taken the Underground from King's Cross to Hammersmith and set off down the street looking for number 161, the address I'd found on the Internet. When I finally spotted the modern red-brick building, I was a little disappointed. I'd hoped to see a nice big sign that I could take a picture of, but there was nothing anywhere that said "St Mungo's". I walked through the revolving doors and over to the reception desk.

According to the floor guide, St Mungo's was on the second floor. I asked the guard if I could take a picture of the sign. Judging by his reaction, not many people ask to take pictures of the floor guide

St Mungo's Hospital for Magical Maladies and Injuries

Location: Central London, near an Underground station, on a busy shopping street.

Function: Hospital which treats the kinds of ailments that only wizards could have, such as Dragon Pox and having one's head turned into a teapot by mistake.

How to get there: A dummy in the window, wearing out-of-date clothes, beckons magical visitors in, who then walk through the window and into the reception.

Description (from the street): A red-brick department store perpetually closed for refurbishment. The store is called Purge and Dowse Ltd.

Description (inside): St Mungo's has six floors. The ground floor is reception, where a harassed blonde 'welcome witch' points patients to the correct floor. There is a tea shop on the fifth floor. The floors in between specialise in various magical ailments, such as malfunctioning spells and bites from magical creatures.

Additional details: Light comes from floating glass balls near the ceiling. Around Christmas, these balls have coloured lights in them. The staff are called Healers and portraits of notable Healers are on the walls. St Mungo's was founded in the 1600s by Mungo Bonham (FW).

for the building. I took the lift up to the second floor and walked into St Mungo's itself. The receptionists were very friendly, nothing like the harassed Welcome Witch in the book. When I explained why I was there, they asked me how their organisation connected to Harry Potter. I told them about the wizarding hospital in the books and asked if I could take a few pictures and they agreed; while I was lining up a shot of the big St Mungo's sign on the wall behind the counter, they asked a little more about the St Mungo's in the books. When they heard that the fictional hospital was filled with witches and wizards, they said they could use a few wizards around their office to help get things done.

FIGURE 30   *The real St Mungo's is on the second floor of this red-brick building on Hammersmith Road*

FIGURE 31
*Reception at St Mungo's...
the REAL St Mungo's*

I thanked them and let them get back to work. As I walked back to the Tube, I thought about where to go next. The St Mungo's I was looking for wasn't going to be as easy to find as this: the book didn't give enough clues to narrow it down to a particular place. I thought about all the buildings being refurbished that I passed as I wandered around London. There are a lot of them. I spotted a particularly good one near Chancery Lane station, made of red brick and covered with scaffolding, but the entire ground floor was covered with plywood so I couldn't see windows at all. I really didn't have much more to go on.

Then, a few weeks later, I got a tip. A friend who had dropped by for a cup of tea made an offhand comment that when she read book five, she remembered a vacant department store on Oxford Street, closed for several years, with mannequins left standing forlornly in the display windows. She couldn't help but wonder if Rowling might have seen that disused store and used the idea for Purge and Dowse Ltd.

Thank goodness for the Internet. It took a little digging to find out what store that was and which building it had occupied, but in the end I discovered that a C&A branch had gone out of business in 2001 and that the building been unoccupied for quite some time. That would have been exactly the period in which Rowling was writing book five, in which we visit St Mungo's. I had to take a look. The building was still there, of course, even though it wasn't abandoned anymore.

Gripping my map, I set out again, taking the bus down to the Centre Point bus stop, where Tottenham Court Road, Oxford Street, Charing Cross Road, and New Oxford Street all come together in what has to be the most annoying intersection in London.

I managed to survive my trek through the intersection, left New Oxford Street behind me and walked down Oxford Street, one of the busiest shopping streets in the city. This would be the perfect place for St Mungo's. Cars and buses rumbled past and I stuck with the crowds dodging traffic across the streets, remembering to look down at the pavement and not make eye contact, since the rule of etiquette in London is that you walk head down and don't look at anyone else. Making eye contact, I'd been warned, is a form of aggression in London.

I always wondered how a group of six people could simply vanish into the display window of St Mungo's Hospital in broad daylight with Muggles all around, but when I was actually walking along the street, it made perfect sense. Purge and Dowse Ltd., as we know from the book, has been closed for refurbishment for years. I found myself darting under scaffolding and around work fences as I walked along. How easy it would be for anyone to walk calmly under just such a scaffold and simply not come out again. No one would notice, I'm sure, since all the other passers-by would be looking at the ground.

FIGURE 32 *On the side street
next to the former C&A store*

According to my research, the old C&A store that my friend had remembered was now an Urban Outfitters. I had walked almost to Oxford Circus before I spotted it, there across the street. The building wasn't red-brick and it was no longer a single store. But the size was right – five storeys tall – and the first-floor windows (that's second floor to us Americans) were still boarded up on the inside with sheets of plywood. Round the side there were plenty of display windows right on the street. I imagined a group of witches and wizards walking up to that building, turning the corner down the side street, and talking to a display dummy there in the windows. Aside from the lack of red brick, it seemed to work pretty well. When I looked around, I saw that I was just a short walk away from the Oxford Circus Underground station. I could easily imagine that Rowling might have come up with her magical hospital idea from seeing this place back in 2001.

It was pretty boring, though, I had to admit. I know that it's *supposed* to seem ordinary and inconspicuous, but I was hoping to find something more. Just what that would be, I couldn't say; but I wanted something to surprise me, the way Lonsdale Square had. I wanted to see something and just know that it was special.

If any city in the world is capable of that kind of surprise, it's London. I walked back the way I came, to the intersection from hell, cowered with a nice group of pedestrians at the light, then scurried over to Tottenham Court Road, going north. To my left and right were electronics shops selling the latest gadgets, all winking and flashing in the windows. Since electronic devices don't work around magical places, I figured I wasn't likely to find a magical hospital on this part of Tottenham Court Road. I turned left onto Goodge Street and kept looking for something, although I still wasn't sure what it would be. Several blocks down, I spotted a very large boarded-up building made of red brick. Walking closer I realised that it was an abandoned hospital. Could St Mungo's actually be there, hiding in plain sight?

I walked along the outside of the boarded-up building, looking up at the vacant windows and wondering if someone suffering from dragon pox or a werewolf bite might be looking back at me. This abandoned hospital, the Middlesex, is actually seven storeys tall, which is two more floors than appear on the St Mungo's floor guide in the book. However, it is quite easy to imagine that the upper floors hide closed wards or potions research rooms. After all, the Wolfsbane Potion had to be invented somewhere. Why not behind one of those empty windows in the garret?

FIGURE 33 *The Middlesex hospital*

MAGICAL MALADIES

Magical maladies are treated on the second floor of St Mungo's Hospital. Two of the most interesting are Dragon Pox and Spattergroit.

✦ Dragon Pox

The symptoms of this disease are quite bizarre, and I'm glad that we Muggles don't suffer from them. In the Daily Prophet newsletters, a certain Howland Coopey writes to the Problem Page describing a 'green and purple rash' between his toes and sparks flying out of his nose when he sneezes. Professor Spleen replies that it's probably Dragon Pox and is likely to go away on its own. We learn from Elphias Doge's account of his own bout of it as a boy that the disease is highly contagious in its early stages, and even after the Pox had run its course, Doge's skin remained green and pocked for some time. According to the Famous Wizard cards, the first known victim of Dragon Pox was a fellow in the 1300s named Chauncery Oldridge. Chapter 3 of *Quidditch Through the Ages*, however, includes a letter written in the 1100s by a wizard named Goodwin Kneen, which mentions that his wife, Gunhilda, missed a Quidditch match because she had contracted Dragon Pox; so perhaps Oldridge was the first person actually to die of the disease. At any rate, the famous Gunhilda of Goresmoor, whose statue stands in a Hogwarts corridor and hides a secret passage to Hogsmeade, developed a cure for Dragon Pox around 1600, about the same time that St Mungo's was founded.

✦ Spattergroit

This very nasty and contagious disease is caused by a fungus. The books don't give us as much background information about Spattergroit, but it does turn up in the stories a couple of times. Once, when Ron Weasley was exploring St Mungo's hospital, a portrait on the wall caught sight of his freckles and told him that he was ill with Spattergroit, offering the cure of pressing a toad's liver to the throat and standing 'naked in a barrel full of eel's eyes' by moonlight. This inspired Ron, in book seven, to disguise the reason he hadn't returned to Hogwarts with Spattergroit, Transfiguring the family ghoul into a rough facsimile of Ron with purple blisters all over his body. When the disease affects the uvula, the sufferer can't even talk, so the Ministry officials who came to check on Ron wouldn't be able to ask him any questions or dare get too close for fear of contagion (OP22).

✦ Other magical maladies and injuries

- ✦ scrofungulus, a very contagious disease (OP22)
- ✦ vanishing sickness, the symptoms of which we can only guess at (OP22)
- ✦ werewolf bite (PA18, OP22) – induces lycanthropy, an incurable condition but controllable with Wolfsbane Potion

A variety of magical maladies are in evidence in the waiting room of St. Mungo's (OP22):

- ✦ small child who had sprouted huge feathery wings
- ✦ man who was wearing jinxed shoes which ate his feet
- ✦ a man whose head rang like a bell whenever he moved it
- ✦ a woman whose head had been made into something like a "teapot" – she whistled and gave off steam, and her face was red and sweaty
- ✦ people with strange things growing out of them, such as an elephant's trunk

FIGURE 34 *Garret window…where Wolfsbane Potion could have been created?*

The massive seven-storey façade beyond the barriers was certainly imposing. I didn't see any display windows to walk through (and certainly no mannequins), but when I walked around to the Cleveland Street side I spotted a beautiful four-storey window that might suffice for a magical entrance. The trouble with that window was that it was about fifteen feet off the ground, and didn't really match the description in the books.

There were plenty of other windows at street level, but they were all separated from the street by iron railings, which made them rather inconvenient for walking through. I stuck my head into a hidden corner around the back of the building, however, and spotted a row of windows covered with plywood which would do nicely for a secret entrance. I pressed my hand against the wood and it was as solid and unyielding as could be. No mannequins beckoned me through, although I did get a few strange looks from the Muggles in hard hats working nearby.

Still, it's a fascinating place. There is something intriguing about a huge stately building like that which is boarded up and inaccessible. What stories could those walls tell, I wondered? It may not be exactly St Mungo's, but it was well worth the walk to see it.

FIGURES 35 & 36
Boarded-up windows, and the disused entrance to the hospital

FIGURE 37 *Façade of the disused hospital*

The Middlesex hospital had been there since the mid-1700s, and was the first hospital in England to have beds for overnight patients. The cornerstone for this building, which now stands boarded up and empty on Mortimer Street, was laid in 1755, some 150 years after the founding of St Mungo's around 1600. According to the records of the Old Bailey, the criminal court in London, plenty of criminals and their victims ended up here over the years, and a fair number never left alive. I could imagine that a few ghosts are still there, wandering the empty hallways.

A GEOGRAPHIC TIMELINE OF
EARLY *HARRY POTTER* HISTORY

Long before Harry Potter was born, events occurred which would define the geography of the wizarding world and also set the stage for his dramatic battles against Lord Voldemort and the Death Eaters. Most of these events, like the ones in the books, are centred around three regions of Britain: the London area, the West Country, and Scotland. Rowling revealed bits of information about this history in a number of places, including the 'Schoolbooks' and in interviews.

c. 1000 BC — Greece: a number of famous witches and wizards lived in this era, the most notable of which was probably Herpo the Foul, arguably the first great Dark Wizard, who created the first Basilisk and invented the horrible magic required to create a Horcrux. Even Herpo never tried to create as many as seven of these terrible Dark Magic items the way Voldemort did.

c. 900 AD — the West Country: Godric Gryffindor is born in a small village which became known years later as Godric's Hollow. This village will feature prominently in the history of the Potter and Dumbledore families.

c. 990 AD — Highlands of Scotland: Hogwarts school is built in the Highlands of Scotland. The school is founded by the four most famous wizards of the age: Godric Gryffindor, Helga Hufflepuff, Rowena Ravenclaw, and Salazar Slytherin. Around the same time, Hengist of Woodcroft founded the village of Hogsmeade nearby. Although the Statute of Secrecy was seven hundred years in the future, the fact that both Hogsmeade and Hogwarts were intentionally founded far away from Muggle civilisation shows that the problems were already underway between the two groups.

c. 1000 AD — Queerditch Marsh, possibly in Devon: Local witches and wizards invent a new game played on broomsticks which involves trying to throw a ball through a goal. The game becomes known as Quidditch, after the place where it was invented. The history of the game is filled with references to the need for keeping the players and spectators hidden away from the Muggle community.

1300s — Godric's Hollow, West Country: A 'metal charmer' named Bowman Wright invents the Golden Snitch, which revolutionised the game of Quidditch (the dates for Wright's life are unclear, since *Quidditch Through the Ages* tells us that the Golden Snitch was created toward the end of the 1300s, but Wright's Chocolate Frog card says he was born in 1492).

1500s — Near St Martin's Lane, outside London: Daisy Dodderidge founds the Leaky Cauldron pub as a waypoint between the Muggle and magical worlds. The pub was originally located in open land, crossed by several paths, where the king's deer roamed. Eventually, the area became part of London; the paths became roads and buildings surrounded the pub. Charing Cross Road now runs past the pub.

c. 1600 — London: St Mungo's Hospital for Magical Maladies and Injuries is founded by Mungo Bonham. Its original location is uncertain, but it is currently housed in a red-brick building in central London, which appears on the outside to be an abandoned department store.

1692 — The Statute of Secrecy goes into effect: Wizarding families band together in or near several Muggle towns where they can live peacefully alongside their Muggle neighbours without drawing undue attention to themselves. These towns include Godric's Hollow, Ottery St Catchpole and Tinworth in the West Country, and Upper Flagley in Yorkshire. Another possible such town is Mould-on-the-Wold, where Dumbledore's family lived when he was very young.

✦ Charing Cross Road ✦
and the Leaky Cauldron

My next destination was the Leaky Cauldron pub. According to the books, this tiny establishment is to be found on Charing Cross Road. That's just a few minutes' walk from the Middlesex hospital, so I headed back towards Tottenham Court Road to see what I could find.

As long as I was on Tottenham Court Road, I thought I'd look around for a grimy little 24-hour coffee shop before I walked to Charing Cross Road. In book seven, when they escaped the Death Eater attack at Bill and Fleur's wedding, Hermione took Harry and Ron to Tottenham Court Road; they attracted unwanted attention from drunken people outside pubs, so they ducked into a coffee shop. I looked around Tottenham Court Road hopefully, but didn't see any coffee shops at all, only shops selling furniture or electronics.

Maybe that was why Hermione took them to that road. As I said before, electronics and magic don't coexist very well, so perhaps she felt that a road full of such shops would act as sort of a damper for anyone trying to track them or, worse yet, cast a spell their way. I walked north along the road, away from the electronics shops, hoping to spot somewhere that might qualify as a grimy café. At

---

NOT-SO-MAGICAL PLACE

24-hour coffee shop

Location: Along Tottenham Court Road.

Function: The place where Harry, Hermione, and Ron hide, and encounter two Death Eaters.

How to get there: Walk down Tottenham Court Road.

Description: "Small and shabby" with a layer of grease on the Formica tabletops.

Additional details: Located fairly near some pubs.

least there were a few coffee shops further north. I saw a Starbucks and other modern, flashy coffee places, but nothing that matched the description in the books.

I thought through the sequence of events in book seven. When they first Apparate away from the wedding, Hermione tells them that they're on Tottenham Court Road, but doesn't say where exactly. After several people laugh at the robes the boys are wearing, she leads them down a side street, then into an alley so they can change. They walk back up the side street and onto the main road again, where a number of drunken men whistle and shout at Hermione. To avoid them, she directs them into a 'small and shabby all-night café'. Two things dawned on me as I thought this through. Firstly, the coffee shop might not be open twenty-four hours, just late into the evening. The fact that it's open late when a lot of other such places are closed might prompt Harry to see it as an 'all-night café'. Secondly, the coffee shop might actually be on another side street; for instance, there's a 24-hour Subway restaurant just around the corner on Oxford Street. If so, the café must still be pretty close to Tottenham Court Road, since Hermione steers them towards it from the main street.

I spotted a possible shop a short way down one side street, near a pub. The coffee shop wasn't open twenty-four hours – not even close, since they close up at 4.30 in the afternoon – but it certainly does fit the kind of grungy café described in the book. It was small, it wasn't particularly fancy, and it was very close to the main road. Maybe this was it.

Well, probably not. It's highly unlikely that Rowling had any particular café in mind when she wrote book seven. Even if she did, whatever grubby café Hermione found back in 1997 when the story took place would likely be long gone now, replaced by Starbucks or Café Nero.

I headed back south towards the intersection from hell, where Tottenham Court Road turns into Charing Cross Road. Having got through that dreadful junction and onto the pavement at the top of Charing Cross Road, I started looking around in earnest. Dominating the intersection is the modern and distinctly non-magical Centre Point building. Could there be witches and wizards

FIGURE 38
*Little coffee shop with
a few tables outside, just
off Tottenham Court
Road, in the background*

all around me? Surely even Muggles would notice folks dressed in cloaks or, worse yet, mismatched and inappropriately colourful clothes. On the other hand, I spotted a fellow striding towards me down New Oxford Street wearing flowered boxer shorts, a multicoloured jumper, pink socks which might have had the Little Mermaid on them, and trainers. He was bearded and carrying a plastic shopping bag. No one even glanced at him. Clearly, he was a wizard, and I could see him just fine even if my fellow Muggles didn't notice him at all. I had hope.

I mentioned before that quiet corners and peaceful squares can be found here and there in London. Charing Cross Road, however, is definitely not one of them: it is as noisy and busy and constantly moving as you can get. Cars and taxis and buses are everywhere, and when they stop for a light or become snarled up for a few moments, pedestrians swarm past and between and through them, all looking at the ground of course. In other words, Charing Cross Road looks and sounds much like every other major street in central London, only more so.

The Leaky Cauldron, according to information on Rowling's website and the Famous Wizard cards she wrote, was founded in the early 1500s by Daisy Dodderidge, to create a connection point between the magical and Muggle worlds; and it is through the Leaky Cauldron that people gain access to Diagon Alley. In book three Harry spends several weeks of pleasant freedom at the Leaky Cauldron after escaping from his Aunt and Uncle's house in Surrey and hitching a ride on the Knight Bus. Yes, that's 'Knight', a takeoff on 'Night Bus', the name for the buses that run through London after midnight.

Somewhere down Charing Cross Road I hoped to find a nondescript pub door that no one notices, nestled between a bookshop and a record store. That's how it was described in the first book. I started walking briskly down the east side of the street, and almost immediately discovered a bookshop. Several bookshops, actually; the further down the road I got, the more bookshops I found. Charing Cross Road is apparently *the* street for bookshops. And Charing Cross Road is also *the* street for music shops, so I found myself surrounded by possible Leaky Cauldron locations.

FIGURE 39 *Busy Charing Cross Road, with the London Hippodrome's rooftop chariot visible across the street*

MAGICAL PLACE

The Leaky Cauldron

Location: Charing Cross Road in central London.

Function: A pub with guest rooms upstairs and a gateway into Diagon Alley out the back.

How to get there: The Leaky Cauldron is between a bookshop and a record shop. The pub is difficult for Muggles to see.

Description (The Leaky Cauldron pub): The Leaky Cauldron is a tiny, 'grubby-looking' pub. Inside is a bar with a number of tables and a corridor leading to a private parlour.

Additional details: The landlord is a 'toothless', wizened old man named Tom.

Sources of information: The Famous Wizard cards

In the interim between books four and five, Rowling found herself managing a growing franchise, and signed deals with a number of companies to produce Harry Potter merchandise. She agreed to let Warner Bros. create the film versions of her books, and chose Electronic Arts to produce Harry Potter video games. In each case she wanted to have input and final say on the various projects that these companies worked on.

The Electronic Arts video games set the player the task of finding about one hundred Famous Wizard cards scattered around the game environment, which were supposed to be similar to the Chocolate Frog cards mentioned in the books. Rowling herself wrote the text for the cards, inventing a large number of new minor characters and a lot of trivial (and not so trivial) details about her world. Many of these Famous Wizard cards turned up later on her website as Wizards of the Month.

As I looked closer, however, I realised that despite seeing more of the requisite types of shops than I could count, I could find no point where a bookshop and a music shop actually sat side by side as described in the books. There were bookshops everywhere, from small shops like the famous Murder Inc. which specialises in mysteries, to big names like Borders and Foyles. They stood side by side, with only the occasional coffee shop or tiny newsagent between them. Towards the north end of Charing Cross Road, a lot of music shops are clustered around the intersection with Denmark Street (although these shops all appeared to sell musical instruments, not records). The problem was that the two types of shop weren't ever right next to each other, as far as I could see. I walked down the street, looking for any place that might hide a magical door.

I was beginning to despair – my Muggle eyes were obviously keeping me from seeing it – when I happened upon a small alcove off the street, with a musical instrument shop on one side and Blackwell's bookshop filling the rest. Between them, partially obscured by potted plants, was a most interesting door.

FIGURE 40
Mysterious door between a music shop and bookshop

FIGURE 4I *The door to the Leaky Cauldron?*

I hadn't even seen it at first, it was so well hidden. An old-fashioned hanging sign swung overhead, the words a bit hard to read at first. I looked again at the mysterious door and realised that it had no handle. This had to be it. I looked left and right and saw the Muggles walking past, eyes averted, oblivious to what I had just found. This could only be a magical door to a magical pub and a passageway to Diagon Alley. I smiled and pressed against the door.

Nothing happened.

I pressed again. Still nothing. I considered knocking but thought better of it.

It was straight out of the books, though: a black door with a hanging sign, partially obscured from sight and ignored by the people on the street. I felt a little thrill of excitement. Somehow, even though I was standing on one of the busiest streets in London, I managed to find something magical, something special.

What was on the other side of that door? Would I be able to buy a magic wand or an owl somewhere beyond its unassuming exterior? Or, better yet, a crystal ball to help me find the magical places I was looking for?

After taking a few pictures, I trudged on down the east side of Charing Cross Road. I had to laugh a little as I looked around me. In the books, a driver of a magical car actually waits along this busy street for several hours while the Weasley family shops in Diagon Alley; I couldn't imagine a car sitting idle anywhere along the road for more than a few moments. There are no parking places on Charing Cross Road. In fact, the outside lane was painted red and restricted to buses only. I suppose the driver could have squeezed the car and himself into a bit of space in the bus lane, but I doubted it; bus drivers don't take kindly to people who park in the bus lanes. But there I was, thinking like a Muggle again. Perhaps the driver simply drove up on the pavement, magically disguised his car as a hot dog wagon or a Thai food stand, and sat hidden in the open.

Everywhere I looked was as mundane and busy and non-magical as could be. The street was noisy and frantic. Ahead of me, people climbed the steps out of Leicester Square Underground station and scurried across the side streets without a glance around them. As I approached the intersection with Cranbourn Street, the driver of a large truck pulled out into Charing Cross Road only to find that he didn't have space to finish his turn without demolishing the railings and a telephone box across the way. He stopped in the middle of the road, cars pressed all around him, and decided to back up and have another go. Not surprisingly, this resulted in a lot of shouting and honking of horns as he inched backwards and forwards. I crossed Cranbourn Street with a huddle of fellow pedestrians and made my way between the cars and taxis, head down, looking at the ground. Ah, the life of a Muggle.

This particular corner did have a magical history to it, although of the Muggle variety. On the corner of Charing Cross Road and Leicester Square is the London Hippodrome, a garish Victorian building with a really cool chariot and horses sculpture on top. The Hippodrome opened in 1900 with a spectacular circus, which featured a huge water tank as part of the show. Circuses have a magic all their own, of course, and the circus in the Hippodrome reportedly included elephants and polar bears and fountains and boats floating in from the side entrances, which would have been something to see. When Harry Houdini performed at the Hippodrome in 1904, he spent over an hour frantically trying to escape from a pair of complicated handcuffs, and the audience was completely enchanted. At the end, he reportedly said it was the most difficult escape of his life. Some say he had actually released himself easily after milking the crowd for an hour, while others suggest that he almost didn't escape at all and that his wife slipped him the key in a glass of water. Either way, a little Muggle magic did occupy this spot on Charing Cross Road a hundred years ago.

✦ Diagon Alley ✦

Diagon Alley was one place I knew I wouldn't be able to find. The only way into Diagon Alley in the books was through a magical gateway in an alley behind the Leaky Cauldron pub. I saw a few small alleyways along Charing Cross Road, but none that had the requisite rubbish bins and brick wall. Since the alley is only accessible through the pub itself, it didn't matter. There was no way to get there, I knew.

Then London surprised me again. I turned a corner from Charing Cross Road and stopped dead in my tracks. My jaw literally dropped. I had found myself in what was surely the most magical alley there could ever be. Hanging signs advertised old books, tarot readings, and collectables. The noises of the street vanished. Amazing. I had found my way into Diagon Alley after all.

The sign on the corner of the street read Cecil Court. Like Diagon Alley, this tiny street nestling between Charing Cross Road and St Martin's Lane was for pedestrians only. The buildings loomed several storeys high on either side, shutting out the noise and craziness of the Muggle world. I walked slowly down the quiet pavement and looked around me.

To my left, I was surprised to see familiar faces. In the small lit window of Martin Murray's shop, which offered coins, stamps, and cigarette cards, was a set of imitation bank notes with the Harry Potter film characters on them. The display placard offered the whole set for £12.50. I was sorely tempted. On the other side of the street was Watkins Esoteric, a shop which advertised tarot card readings. They sold crystals, candles, and various other items that one would be sure to find in a Diagon Alley shop.

Cecil Court is home to some of the most intriguing and, yes, magical bookshops I could ever imagine. There are shops specialising in first editions, in children's and illustrated books, and in antique and rare books. Flourish and Blott's, the bookshop in Diagon Alley, would be right at home here next to David Drummond's, a shop specialising in theatre memorabilia, Victorian postcards and, to my delight, books about conjuring and magic.

FIGURE 42
Cecil Court

FIGURE 43
Shops in Cecil Court

One shop in particular caught my eye and I stopped in front of the display window, completely enchanted. The shop owner's name, Mark Sullivan, is printed overhead and on the hanging sign, and he sells, as he puts it, "eclectic items and unusual objects". That description simply can't convey the wonder of his premises. Even before I walked through the door, I had spotted the crystal ball I'd been hoping to buy among the bits and bobs in the display window. In the corner stood a figurine of a wizard in a pointed hat. Tiny boxes, antique cameras, portraits, ceramics, telescopes, and delicate cups were among the myriad of items crammed into the window. I had to explore further.

MAGICAL PLACE

Diagon Alley

Location: In magical space behind the Leaky Cauldron on Charing Cross Road.

Function: A magical High Street of shops for witches and wizards, the centre of commerce for the magical community.

How to get there: In the small courtyard behind the Leaky Cauldron, tap the bricks of the wall with a wand in a particular pattern. The bricks melt away to reveal a gateway into Diagon Alley.

Description: The street is cobbled and usually filled with people. Some shops, like the cauldron shop, pile their wares outside their doors in the street.

Some of the main shops: Gringott's Wizarding Bank, Flourish and Blott's bookshop, Weasley's Wizard Wheezes joke shop, Madam Malkin's Robes for All Occasions, Ollivander's wand shop, Eeylops Owl Emporium, The Magical Menagerie, Florean Fortesque's Ice Cream Parlour, and Quality Quidditch Supplies.

Additional details: Knockturn Alley, a road which connects to Diagon Alley near Gringotts, sells Dark Magic supplies and items.

Inside was more, so much more that I couldn't take it all in. I was convinced that if I had a shopping list of things I need to buy for Hogwarts like the one Harry received in book one, I could find everything I needed somewhere in Mark Sullivan's amazing shop. There were tiny books smaller than a credit card. A rack held canes and walking sticks of every sort, somewhere among which was probably a magic wand or two. In a glass display case, nestled between a cameo brooch and some tarnished silver spoons, lay an old, innocent-looking locket. In the wall case behind me, beneath a row of old mugs and a bust of Winston Churchill, was a collection of glass chemical bottles that almost certainly held potions. And best of all, on a top shelf stood a small stuffed owl with white feathers. I spent a long time in Mark's shop. Like Harry on his first visit to Diagon Alley, I wished I had about eight more eyes.

Eventually I walked back out into Cecil Court and looked into other shop windows. Immediately I spotted a display of old maps, prominent among which was a map of London dated from the 1600s. That was not long after the time when Daisy Dodderidge founded the Leaky Cauldron. I looked closer, matching the antique map to the arrangement of streets I knew, and orientated myself. There, where Charing Cross Road is now, were open fields crisscrossed with paths. One of them might just be where Cecil Court is now. In fact, I learned later that, though its currrent buildings had been put up in the nineteenth century, Cecil Court itself had been laid out in the late 1600s. One of those paths on the map was undoubtedly the street I was on. When Daisy would have opened the Leaky Cauldron, it would have been located on a small lane and surrounded by fields. Over the centuries, the city grew up around it. I wondered what the area would have looked like when the Leaky Cauldron was built.

I stopped into a few more shops and chatted with the proprietors. It was clear that I wasn't the only person to feel the magic of this place. I heard fond stories of old books found in unusual places and tales of hidden passageways under the shops, and learned that Cecil Court had once been the home to a range of establishments

FIGURES 44 & 45 *Inside Mark Sullivan's shop: a most amazing array of things for sale. (Inset) Potions bottles?*

FIGURE 46
*Antique maps
for sale*

FIGURE 47
*One of several
bookshops in
Cecil Court*

of varying degrees of respectability, including a brandy shop where the customers were described in old court records as "drinking, smoaking, and swearing, and running up and down Stairs till one or two in the Morning".

All such shenanigans are gone these days, although one can find a bite to eat and a bottle of wine in the Indian restaurant on the corner with St Martin's Lane. The shops of Cecil Court now offer pleasures of a different, more refined kind. More than that, they offer what can only be described as magic in a tiny street off Charing Cross Road.

But one more surprise awaited me as I left the far end of Cecil Court and crossed St Martin's Lane. A small doorway on the far side of the street bore the sign 'Goodwin's Court'. I thought about it for a moment, and then figured hey, why not? I ducked through.

Was I ever glad I did. Goodwin's Court is a short, narrow alley that runs between St Martin's Lane and Bedfordbury. Unlike Cecil Court, which was completely rebuilt in the late 1800s, the buildings of Goodwin's Court date back to the 1600s. Very likely,

FIGURE 48
Goodwin's Court

as the city gradually replaced the open fields around the Leaky Cauldron, the streets would have looked something like this. The buildings facing each other on either side of the street are extremely close together and the windows on the ground floor bow outward. The street lamps are gas, and still work from the looks of them. The doors are polished black wood with brass knobs in the centre. I walked the short distance from one end of the Court to the other and half expected Sherlock Holmes to stride past me at any moment. Most of the premises in the Court are offices, however, and it was a bit jarring to glance in the windows and see computers and other accoutrements of a modern office behind such an old-fashioned façade. There were no shops in Goodwin's Court, and only one restaurant, Giovanni's, down on the end by Bedfordbury. I walked back out, crossed to Cecil Court and hurried back to Charing Cross Road to catch the bus.

I tried to imagine how a magical establishment like the Leaky Cauldron would change and adapt to the Muggle world around it. The little inn that Daisy Dodderidge founded would have most likely been standing all on its own along a lane in open fields back in the 1600s. I tried to imagine a series of images of the pub, say one every ten years, as the landscape changed around it. Diagon Alley was safe, since it would presumably exist in some alternative magical space, rather like Platform Nine and Three-Quarters. But what about the Leaky Cauldron itself? As the Muggle streets and shops were built, remodelled, and replaced over the years, would the magical building just remain, unchanged?

Of course, this is all just part of a story and Rowling probably never thought about how that would happen, but it's fun to think about, especially after seeing the contrasts between Goodwin's Court, Cecil Court, and Charing Cross Road. I thought about a trip I'd taken to Leeds where I had turned off from the modern and bustling high street down a narrow passageway to discover a three-hundred-year old pub still doing business, hidden behind the more modern buildings which had been built right around it. That's how I imagine the Leaky Cauldron, tucked away behind the shops and restaurants, accessible through a single, inconspicuous door. A black one, with just a simple hanging sign and maybe a few potted palms.

✦ The Ministry of Magic ✦

A phone box. That was next. A phone box in a side street near a couple of dumpsters, or 'skips' as they are called in Britain. At first I thought this one would be fairly easy to find. There are phone boxes all over the place in London. I just had to find one by some dumpsters.

I had two different ideas about where to look. First of all, I like the idea of the Ministry of Magic being located near the government buildings in London, which are clustered around Westminster and Victoria. But secondly, the book says that Harry and Mr Weasley walk a little way from the Tube stop and that the streets get less impressive as they go. A few years ago, a fan had emailed that they'd seen a likely phone box in Aldwych, near Waterloo Bridge. That seemed as good a place as any to start, so I took the bus to the Strand and set out. Very near the place I got off the bus I found the phone box standing next to a police station. While it was situated a little way from the main road on the intersection of two side streets, it was hardly in an area of 'less imposing' buildings. There are certainly no skips anywhere around, either. I decided to continue searching elsewhere, and headed off towards Buckingham Palace and the Houses of Parliament.

FIGURE 49 *Phone box next to a police station, near the Strand*

I saw plenty of phone boxes, but every one I saw as I walked around was right on a busy street. It makes sense, I suppose, since no one would use a phone box that's tucked away out of sight in a dingy side street. There are phone boxes near Big Ben and next to Westminster Abbey, but these areas are completely skip-free, just like the area around the police station. I did find a public lavatory,

---

MAGICAL PLACE

The Ministry of Magic

Location: Central London, but a bit off the beaten track, since Harry and Mr Weasley walk from the Underground station into an area of 'less imposing' buildings before coming to a street with a few offices, a phone box, and a skip.

Function: Offices of the government of the magical community.

How to get there: Most witches and wizards use the Floo Network of fireplaces to travel into the Ministry. The huge atrium on the ninth floor is lined with fireplaces for this purpose. The visitors' entrance is a telephone box on the street above, next to some skips. A witch or wizard enters the box and dials 62442, is asked politely for the nature of their business, then is issued with a name badge and transported downwards under the street.

Description: The Ministry of Magic is a huge complex located entirely underground. There are eleven levels. Level nine is the Atrium, until recently dominated by a statue of a witch and wizard surrounded by a centaur, a house-elf, and a goblin. Level ten consists of courtrooms. The Department of Mysteries is on level eleven, but the lifts don't go down that far.

Additional details: During the year when Voldemort took over the Ministry, employees had to enter the Ministry through public lavatories on the street above, by standing in the toilet bowl and flushing themselves down. Magical Maintenance is responsible for the weather seen through the enchanted windows. When angling for a pay rise at one point, they reportedly set the windows to show hurricanes.

however, which just could be the lavatory that Ministry employees were forced to use to get to work during the takeover by Death Eaters. I took a few pictures of the lavatories, keenly aware of the fact that my British friends would tease me for taking pictures of loos. Tourists will take pictures of anything, they laugh. Well, they're right. I set off again, looking for some skips to photograph next.

FIGURE 50 *Phone box near Big Ben*

FIGURE 51
A photo I snapped of public lavatories near Westminster Abbey, proof that tourists will take pictures of anything

The part of London I was exploring is grand and impressive. The buildings are designed to inspire. I walked past Buckingham Palace and couldn't help but wonder whether the guards in their tall bearskin hats would be allowed to take those hats off if they actually were called upon to defend the palace. If not, they'd have a tough time hiding behind anything: the hat would stick up and give them away. A few weeks later, I happened to meet a fellow who had been one of those guards, now working as security at a hotel. He told me that no matter what, the hats stay on. Even if you have to run, I asked him? He looked at me sharply and told me in no uncertain terms that he would *never* run. I think he assumed I was questioning his bravery.

The only intrusion into the palace grounds that I saw was a horse-drawn carriage pulling up and dropping someone off. It might have been the Prime Minister. I have heard rumours that he goes to tea with the Queen one afternoon every week. I couldn't really tell if the man climbing out of the carriage was him, since I wasn't sure what Gordon Brown looks like and it was way across the courtyard. The carriage was cool, though; if I was Prime Minister, I might want to ride around in it. I'd rather ride around in an Aston Martin, of course, but I doubt I'll ever have a chance to do either.

At any rate, I wandered further, peering down every side street and thinking about fancy cars and furry hats. Near St James's Park Underground station, I spotted a few skips down an alley and realised that there was a phone box fairly close. I couldn't get both the phone box and the alley in the same shot, but I took a few pictures anyway, just in case.

FIGURE 52 *A phone box near St James's Park Underground Station…*

FIGURE 53 *…and the alley nearby with a skip at the far end*

FIGURE 54
Finally, phone boxes near some skips on a side street!

I made for Victoria Street for no particular reason and realised that I was only a block or two from the offices of my publisher, Methuen. I hadn't chatted with them for a while, so I turned down a side street, looking for Artillery Row. I focused on finding my way where I was going and of course, looking at the pavement.

Suddenly I stopped dead in my tracks. There along the side of this out-of-the-way street was a pair of phone boxes and, to my surprise, a row of skips close by. I looked around, delighted. The street I was on was one of those in London where market stalls are set up during the day, and it was noisy and messy and full of people. The buildings on either side were ordinary and unimposing.I looked back at the phone boxes and the skips. This had to be it! I took picture after picture while the people around glanced up in surprise then walked past, looking rather pointedly at the ground. Little did they know that this phone booth in a dingy side street could be the doorway to a magical world.

After taking a slew of pictures, I went around the corner to say hello to my friends at Methuen and told them happily that I'd found the entrance to the Ministry of Magic right nearby. And, I went on excitedly, I had taken pictures of a skips! What a great place London was, I exclaimed. I'm not sure they were impressed.

3

THE WEST COUNTRY

In the dark of an August night, Harry Potter found himself travelling across the south of England from Surrey to Devon in a flying car. For me, it was a rented Renault and the M5 motorway. I hoped, however, to end up in the same place Harry did: the Weasleys' home, the Burrow, in the West Country.

As I mentioned, much of the saga of Harry Potter takes place in three areas of Britain. I had explored one of those places: London and the county of Surrey nearby. The second location for the stories was Hogwarts, which was found far to the north in Scotland. Before taking a journey north, I turned my attention to the West Country, the other region featured in the books. The West Country is the large rural area extending all the way from the middle of southern England to the westernmost point of Cornwall. It consists of the counties of Avon, Bristol, Cornwall, Devon, Dorset, and Somerset. Gloucestershire and Wiltshire are usually considered to be part of the West Country as well.

The West Country, according to the novels, has been a haven for witches and wizards since at least the end of the 1600s. Here, as Hermione informs Harry in book seven, magical communities were formed as wizarding families banded together near Muggle towns for mutual support and protection. Although the towns Hermione identifies in her reading of *A History of Magic* don't appear on any real maps of the area, all but one of those places are said to be located in the West Country. According to the *A History of Magic* Tinworth, where Bill and Fleur Weasley's home, Shell Cottage, sits on a bluff overlooking the sea, is found in Cornwall; while Ottery St Catchpole, where the Weasley family home is located, is found along the south-west coast of England. Perhaps the most important village of all is Godric's Hollow, which the book refers to simply as a "West Country village".

Wiltshire, part of the West Country nearer to London, is the location of Malfoy Manor, where Voldemort set up his headquarters for the Second Wizarding War in books six and seven. Perhaps that explains why a disaster at the beginning of book six involving

MAGICAL PLACES

West Country

Wiltshire: Malfoy Manor is located in Wiltshire. Voldemort set up his headquarters here in the Second Wizarding War.

Tinworth: Bill and Fleur Weasley's Shell Cottage is located on the coast of Cornwall near Tinworth. It was used as a safe house during the war against Voldemort.

Ottery St Catchpole: The Burrow, the family home of the Weasleys, is located just a short way to the south of the town of Ottery St Catchpole.

The moors: There are a number of moors in the West Country, the most prominent being Bodmin Moor in Cornwall and Exmoor and Dartmoor in Devon. Professional Quidditch stadiums are located on the moors.

Queerditch Marsh: This boggy place, possibly in Devon, was where the game of Quidditch was invented a thousand years ago.

Godric's Hollow: A small village which is the birthplace of Harry Potter and the location of the house where his parents were killed.

Somerset: A giant attack in Somerset was passed off by the Muggles as a hurricane. There's a Snidget Reservation somewhere in the county.

uprooted trees and damage to buildings took place in Somerset, just to the south-west of Wiltshire. The Muggle Prime Minister was quite sure it was caused by a freak hurricane, but Cornelius Fudge, the erstwhile Minister for Magic, explained to him that it was almost certainly a giant. That gave the Prime Minister a turn.

Wiltshire is a particularly interesting place for the Malfoy home. The countryside is dotted with ancient monuments and mysterious sites. Salisbury Plain, a large plateau, is noted for ancient burial mounds and Iron Age stone forts, as well as the famous Stonehenge, a prehistoric circle of standing stones. On a few hillsides, stark white outlines of horses can be seen, created by the removal of the turf to reveal the chalk beneath. Elsewhere in Wiltshire is Silbury Hill, a fascinating, enigmatic mound created more than four thousand years ago, which stands 130 feet high in an almost perfect cone. In Rowling's magical world, one can easily imagine that many of these weird and mysterious places have connections to witches and wizards.

Wiltshire is also famous for crop circles, complicated patterns created in fields by flattening the crops and visible most clearly from the air. In the Harry Potter books, these circles are created in one of two ways: by a shy magical creature called a Mooncalf, which dances in fields in the nighttime on its large flat feet, or by wizards competing in the "Contorting Cereals" division of the Annual International Wizard Gardening Competition. Clearly, Wiltshire is a very magical place.

Of the towns mentioned as being in the West Country, neither Tinworth nor Ottery St Catchpole exists on any Muggle map of Devon and Cornwall. I could make a few educated guesses about their location, however. A good possibility for Tinworth would be Tintagel, famous for its connection to the King Arthur stories. On a rocky promontory jutting out into the sea stand the ruins of an ancient castle, which was supposedly the place where Arthur was conceived and also the location of his final battle with Mordred. I could easily imagine Rowling making a veiled connection to that legendary place, especially since there is a fascinating Museum of Witchcraft in Boscastle, just up the road. However, in book seven Harry watches the sun come up over the sea as he looks out of the kitchen window of Shell Cottage; Tintagel is located on the north-west coast of Cornwall, so there is no possible way for a sunrise to be seen over the sea there.

The coastline of Cornwall does face more or less to the east near Penzance. From Lizard Point all the way past Falmouth to St. Austell, the coastline also offers plenty of places where a cottage on the cliffs would have a view of the sunrise. There are no towns along that coast with a name similar to Tinworth, but there are plenty of cliffs overlooking the sea. Picturesque towns are tucked away in tiny coves all along the coast, with whitewashed houses and even some thatched roofs. Shell Cottage could easily be hidden away along those cliffs.

If it weren't for the fact that it's in Devon, not Cornwall, a good match would be Teignmouth, located along the south Devon coast just south of Dawlish. Teignmouth, pronounced 'TIN-mouth', was once a very busy port and popular holiday destination and there are

MAGICAL PLACE

Shell Cottage

Location: Near Tinworth in Cornwall, on a bluff looking east over the sea.

Function: The home of Bill and Fleur Weasley.

How to get there: Broomstick or Apparition, although there is very likely also a road of some kind.

Description (outside): A 'whitewashed' cottage with shells 'embedded' in its walls, in a small garden with flowerbeds outlined in white stones.

Description (inside): The house is not large – the upstairs has just three small bedrooms, and downstairs there is only a modest kitchen and a sitting room with a fireplace – but it's very pleasant and inviting.

Additional details: Shell Cottage serves as a safe house during the Second Wizarding War. At one time, Bill, Fleur, Harry, Ron, Hermione, Dean Thomas, Luna Lovegood, Griphook and Mr Ollivander were all staying there. Dobby the House-Elf is buried in the garden under a white stone.

spectacular red sandstone cliffs along the coast in that area, facing east over the English Channel. With so few clues, however, I can't narrow it down much closer than that.

Ottery St Catchpole is a bit easier to locate. In Devon there is a town called Ottery St Mary, so named because it is located along the River Otter; so I explored maps of that area and discovered a number of other names which had appeared in the books, altered slightly. Chudleigh was most likely the home of the Quidditch team called the Chudley Cannons. This is Ron Weasley's favourite team, and sure enough, it's located quite near Ottery St Mary. The seaside town of Dawlish, just up the coast from Teignmouth, gave its name to an Auror – a Dark Wizard fighter working for the Ministry of Magic – and Budleigh Salterton appeared as Budleigh Babberton, the Muggle town where Slughorn hid in book six.

Why did Rowling include so many references to this region in the books? One obvious reason is that she went to the University of Exeter back in the 1980s, so the names and places were probably well known to her. She had grown up in Gloucestershire, the northernmost county of the West Country – indeed the Gloucestershire town of Dursley, which Rowling hated visiting as a child, was to lend its name to Harry's loathsome relatives.

Another reason, however, is that the West Country is largely rural, with numerous small towns and villages tucked away in the rolling hills. Many of these towns retain the charm of the England of centuries past, and have a long history of legends and tales that predate the ancient buildings and byways. What better place could there be for witches and wizards to live in seclusion and safety, far from the modern world of motorways and housing estates?

There is one more interesting connection to the West Country in the Harry Potter books. The game of Quidditch, according to *Quidditch Through The Ages*, was first played in a place called Queerditch Marsh, which is where the sport got its name. In north Devon there is a town named Quoditch. Like most of Devon, the area around Quoditch is farmland. Near the town is the small Quoditch Moor Nature Reserve, which is privately held and maintained and is not open to the public. Quoditch Moor is an area of several connected fields comprised of "culm grassland", former fields which

FIGURE 55 *Quoditch Moor in summer* (*image courtesy Viridian Photography*)

are perpetually damp and soggy. The nature reserve is home to a great variety of insects, plants, and animals. The owners told me that they don't know the full history of the land, but that a map from the 1800s shows their small section of land as forest even though all the fields around it are ploughed.

It's not hard to imagine that an area like this, wet and boggy and poorly suited for farming, could have been the marsh where Gertie Keddle drank nettle tea, watched her neighbours playing a silly game on their broomsticks, and wrote angry diary entries about their ball landing in her cabbages. It's also plausible that Rowling, who collected names and words and used many of them in her books, remembered the name Quoditch when she was inventing the name of her magical sport.

FIGURE 56
Quoditch Moor in Devon
(*image courtesy Viridian Photography*)

✦ Ottery St Catchpole ✦

Of all the wizarding places in the West Country, I figured that Ottery St Catchpole would be the easiest to find. After all, the name seemed to be borrowed with some alteration from the very real town of Ottery St Mary, located a few miles from Exeter. Why might the town in the book, Ottery St Catchpole, be the same as Ottery St Mary? Perhaps Rowling simply borrowed the name but imagined her fictional town somewhere else. It's possible, of course, but not likely. The first part of the name of the town comes from the River Otter which flows through this part of Devon to the sea; there isn't any other River Otter in Britain, so the fictional town almost certainly lies somewhere along that river. Rowling was familiar with the area, and the countryside fits the descriptions in the book; plus the books say that Ottery St Catchpole is on the southern coast of England, and Ottery St Mary is only about five miles from the sea.

My trip from London started on the motorways, what Americans would call freeways. British motorways are every bit as unmagical as their counterparts in Europe and America. The first part of the journey took me through modern cities and suburbs, not the sort of place you would expect to find a magical little village or hidden farm. However, the landscape changed as I travelled further west, cities and suburbs giving way to rolling farmland and trees.

I left the motorway at Exeter, took the A30 for a couple of miles, and then turned off at the interestingly-named town of Hand and Pen. From there I followed a road that wound through fields and between hedgerows and lines of trees towards Ottery St Mary. Occasionally in the distance I could see the Devon countryside. Much of the time, however, I couldn't see anything but the road – these lanes are all hemmed in by hedgerows and impenetrable walls of trees and bushes, behind which it would be surprisingly easy to hide all sorts of interesting things.

I was looking for the Burrow, a small farm, hidden among these hills and fields, home to the Weasley family. According to the books, the Burrow is quite near Ottery St Catchpole, since on the morning of the Quidditch World Cup in book four, Harry and some of the

FIGURE 57 *A Devon road*

Weasley family had walked from the Burrow through the town and beyond to a hill called Stoatshead. I knew that I'd have to poke around in the surrounding countryside to find a likely place – at one point in the books, Molly Weasley mentioned that she wasn't sure that the Muggle postman even knew where their house was. But before I started tramping through the fields to find a likely spot for the Burrow, I wanted to explore Ottery St Mary.

I arrived in a delightful town of little shops and meandering streets. Directly in my path was the Volunteer Inn, where I stopped in for a pint and a chat – if there were any interesting goings-on in this small town, someone in the pub would be able to tell me about it.

After drawing me a pint of lager and hearing that I was in search of magical places, the fellow behind the bar asked me if I knew about the Tar Barrels: every year on or near the Fifth of November, known in Britain as Guy Fawkes Night, men of the town set fire to barrels of tar and run through the streets with them held on their heads. As he described this and showed me pictures, I couldn't help but recall some of the strange sports Rowling describes in *Quidditch Through the Ages*. One of Rowling's more dangerous invented broom sports was called Aingingein, supposedly played in Ireland, in which barrels were placed on high stilts and set ablaze. The players would use the gallbladder of a goat as a ball, which was called the Dom, and fly on their brooms through the barrels, one after the other. The point of the game was to throw the Dom through the final barrel without catching on fire. Though there is no Dom in the Tar Barrel spectacle in Ottery St Mary, it's not hard to imagine where Rowling's idea may have come from – the men carrying the barrels are certainly in danger of setting themselves on fire as they move through the crowd.

Unfortunately, I arrived in the town a few weeks after Guy Fawkes Night, so I didn't get to see the Tar Barrels celebration for myself; I made a mental note to come down another year and join in the fun. The evening ends in a huge bonfire, which would also be quite something to see. The Guy Fawkes Night fireworks I had attended a few weeks before in North London were some of the best I've ever seen, but they didn't have a bonfire. Maybe next year I will do the thing properly and spend the weekend in Ottery St Mary.

If I can't manage a trip in November, I might instead want to visit the town around Midsummer's Day, June 24. On the Saturday nearest to that date, the town suffers a 'plague of pixies', in which costumed groups of local children re-enact a legendary event from 1454, when the bells of the church of St Mary were hung and rang out for the first time. Back then, according to the local legend, the town was ruled by the pixies, who caused no end of trouble and disruption, as pixies tend to do. The sound of the church bells ringing drove the pixies away and they fled to nearby caves known as the Pixie's Parlour. Every year now, the children playing the pixies run about the town, trying to capture the bell ringers from the church and keep the bells from ringing. In the end, of course, the pixies fail and the bells ring out. The celebration ends with fireworks in the park as the pixies are once again banished from the town.

A PORLOCK ENCOUNTER?

One of the most famous mysteries from the West Country is sometimes referred to as The Devil's Walk. In the winter of 1855, after a heavy overnight snowfall, the residents of towns to the south and east of Exeter awoke to find a strange set of footprints crossing their fields and farms. From accounts at the time, the tracks seemed to travel in a straight line over houses and walls, stopping mysteriously on one side of a haystack and continuing on the other side, and even stopping at the edge of a two-mile-wide river only to pick up again on the far bank. All told, the tracks were said to cover a hundred miles of countryside.

The footprints were analyzed and drawn in detail. There were not actually very large, no more than an inch or two across, and about eight inches apart. Whatever had made them must have been quite small. They were determined to be made by hoofs, but that the creature making them had walked upright, not on all fours. It didn't take long for many people to exclaim that the Devil himself had walked through their streets and fields, although given the evidence, he would have to have been a lot smaller than one might expect.

Of course, scientifically-minded folks at the time came up with explanations which relied more on genuine observations and less on hysteria. Various animals were suggested as the source; even the description of hoof prints was questioned because any sort of print made in heavy snow is likely to look like simply a round hole and not show a lot of detail.

However, that really doesn't matter. The mystery of the Devil's Walk is very much a part of the local folklore. Rowling would have probably heard the tale when she lived in that area. She borrowed a lot of things from the Devon countryside for the Harry Potter books, including the names of towns (Dawlish, for example); it's very possible that she also included her own sly reference to this mysterious legend in the creature she calls a Porlock.

According to *Fantastic Beasts and Where to Find Them*, the Porlock is a small, hoofed, hairy magical creature, standing about two feet tall when fully grown, that lives on farms in Dorset, which is adjacent to Devon on the south coast of England. The Porlock is a 'horse guardian' and will live in a stable near the horses. Porlocks are very shy and will hide when Muggles come around.

Maybe, on a wintry night back in 1855, a Porlock found himself lost in Devon and left his unusual tracks in the snow as he ran across the landscape, looking for a way back to his farm and his horses.

✦ The Burrow ✦

As I planned this trip, I thought about which way to go from Ottery St Mary. It took some digging, but I worked it out eventually: in the fourth book, when Harry and the Weasleys set out from the Burrow to walk through the town, they see the sun coming up to their right, which would suggest that the Burrow is more or less to the south of Ottery St Catchpole, the book's version of the town. How's that for picking out obscure details?

MAGICAL PLACE

The Burrow

Location: A mile or two outside of the Muggle town of Ottery St Catchpole.

Function: The magical home of the Weasley family.

How to get there: The house is hidden away pretty well, but there must be a road that leads to it because two Muggle taxis show up in the yard.

Description (outside and yard): The Burrow is a ramshackle home, built haphazardly and 'held up by magic'. It has a number of chimneys and a red roof. A rusty cauldron and other odds and ends litter the yard. The garden is tangled and overgrown, and is infested with gnomes – real gnomes, not the little statues you see in Muggle gardens.

Description (inside): The Burrow is a rather small and cramped, but bursting with magic. The dishes wash themselves, magical clocks and devices are all over the place, and strange noises come from the attic where the ghoul lives. The ground floor consists of the kitchen and sitting room. The staircase is narrow and uneven. The four upper floors consist of bedrooms. Ron's room is on the top floor.

Additional details: The Burrow is located to the south of the village. On the opposite side of Ottery St Catchpole is Stoatshead Hill, where Harry and the Weasleys found a Portkey to take them to the Quidditch World Cup.

So I drove south. Of course it's very unlikely that Rowling had a particular spot on the map in mind when she wrote the book; however, I had to start somewhere. The Burrow in the book would be somewhere among the farms and fields to the south of town.

About a mile down the narrow road I came to the small hamlet of Wiggaton. My GPS indicated a road off to the left, so I turned. Once past a few buildings, I found myself on an extremely narrow lane, completely hedged in with trees and bushes. I couldn't really see much around me at all. I passed the signs for a couple of farms and then, as I rolled over a hill and down into a woods, I saw a signpost ahead. To my complete astonishment, the sign pointing left read 'Burrow ¼'.

I stopped in the middle of the lane and stared. I could scarcely believe what I was seeing. I got out of the car and took a few pictures in the fading light. I walked to the sign and looked left where it was pointing. There was another lane there, even narrower than the one I was on, hemmed in by trees and overgrown bushes. This road, if I could call it that, went downhill and disappeared into the wood.

For a moment, I wondered if I even dared drive down that road. Would there be a place to turn around if I got stuck? But I couldn't turn back now. I got back into the car and drove down the tiny road towards the Burrow.

A quarter of a mile later, I saw an overgrown wall along the left side of the road. Beyond that I could see a house with a thatched roof and an open gate, and as I got closer, I spotted the name on the wall: Burrow Hill Farm. I got out of the car, walked up to the gate, and peeked in.

The farmyard was small. The farm buildings were old and somewhat lopsided, but they were painted a clean white and obviously well maintained. I saw a man working at the far end of the yard and decided not to intrude, so took a few pictures through the open gate then got back in the car. The only way I could figure to turn around was to pull into the drive a little, then back up. As I did this, the man came running, shouting for me to stop. As it transpired, I was inches away from rolling the car into a concealed ditch on the far side of the road. Once he had guided my car out of danger, the man introduced himself as the owner of the farm. I thanked him profusely, then asked

FIGURES 58 & 59 *A surprising signpost points down a narrow lane*

FIGURE 60 *Burrow Hill Farm*

if he'd mind me taking a few pictures in the farmyard. He agreed, slightly taken aback; it was quite ramshackle, he admitted. Well of course it is, I thought happily, it's the Burrow after all, and followed him through the gate.

I was standing in the yard of the Burrow. I didn't see any chickens scurrying around nor any discarded boots or cauldrons near the door as described in the books. In fact, Burrow Hill Farm was completely charming. I took pictures of the buildings and the house, trying not to show how excited I was to be there. The farmer said I was welcome to take all the pictures I liked as long as I wasn't casing the place for a robbery or anything. I assured him that I was just looking for magical places hidden away in Britain; he warmed to that and told me that often folks will move into these old farms and try to modernise them, but he was intent on keeping the place the way it is. I hope he does. The farm is delightful. It really could be the Burrow.

It's true that the house wasn't five or six storeys high like the Burrow in the books, but then the original owner didn't have the advantage of magic to hold it all up. The roofs of both the house and the barn were thatch. Flowerpots, implements and buckets were lined up along

FIGURES 61–64 *Burrow Hill Farm*
From left to right: the house, the farmyard, the barn and the gateway

the walls. A few vehicles were parked around the yard, although there were no Ford Anglias.

Between the house and an outbuilding, a small opening caught my eye, and I walked over and looked through. Beyond was the most beautiful view of Devon countryside that I could ever imagine. A fence enclosed the paddock behind the house, and beyond that were copses and rolling green hills. In my mind's eye I saw the Weasley children loping down the slope towards the clearing in the nearest patch of woods to play a rousing match of two-a-side Quidditch, safely out of view of any Muggles who might be nearby.

I could scarcely believe that I was actually standing in the yard of the Burrow. I wondered if Rowling had seen this on a map or heard it mentioned somewhere. Could it be just a coincidence that there was actually a farm called The Burrow a mile south of Ottery St Mary?

It was getting dark. I thanked the owner again for rescuing me and for letting me take pictures, then climbed back into the car; it was time to head back to the Muggle world of the motorway. As I drove off, I noticed to my surprise that my GPS device had stopped working. All it showed was a blank screen. I hoped I would be able to find my way back through the dark lanes. But I shouldn't have been surprised. After all, Muggle electronics never work around magical places.

FIGURE 65 *The Devon countryside beyond the Burrow*

MAGICAL CREATURES OF OTTERY ST CATCHPOLE

The Weasleys raise chickens and the garden pond is full of frogs, but according to the books, a number of magical creatures also live in and around the Burrow.

Gnomes – These small, ugly creatures live underground and among the plants of the garden of the Burrow. Every so often, the Weasley children are assigned the chore of 'de-gnoming' the garden, which involves catching the little gnomes by the ankles, swinging them around a few times to disorientate them, and flinging them as far as possible over the fence, where they march away disconsolately. They always come back, though.

Ghoul – In the attic of the Burrow lives the family ghoul. It's lumpy and smelly and likes to make odd noises from time to time, but it's harmless.

Freshwater Plimpies – These odd little fish, round as a ball with long webbed legs, live in the streams around Ottery St Catchpole, or so Luna Lovegood's father told Harry, Ron, and Hermione when they visited during the Christmas holidays.

✦ The Moors ✦

My next destination was a little village in north Devon called Shebbear. I left Ottery St Mary the next morning and headed north-west. The route I'd chosen took me along Dartmoor. This wasn't the shortest route to Shebbear, but according to Rowling, professional Quidditch stadiums are located on the moors, so I took a detour to take a look.

I had never been to a moor before. I had a vague impression of a large open area of uninhabited wilderness, but as I drove toward Dartmoor I realised that 'large' was an understatement. The moor rose in the distance like a wide, flat mountain. I drove a road that climbed higher and higher out of the Devon farmlands until I found myself in one of the most intriguing and strangely beautiful landscapes I could imagine. There were no trees, although the gorse bushes at times stood almost as tall. The ground was smooth and covered with pale green vegetation. The gently rolling hills rose to sharp points here and there. These points, called tors, were each topped with a cluster of grey stones.

I decided to explore further. A tor nearby seemed a likely destination, so I left the car in a parking area and set off on foot.

FIGURE 66 *Dartmoor in the distance*

As soon as I left the tarmac I discovered that the moor wasn't as smooth as I had thought. The vegetation was thick under my shoes and the same grey stone that dominated the tor ahead was scattered everywhere, to be stepped over or around. Unexpectedly I encountered a stream running through a small gully. The rocks were even more exposed near the stream and made for a convenient, if somewhat treacherous, bridge across the water. But the ground on either side was soggy, as if the stream actually ran through the land surrounding it, not just over.

In fact, as I was to learn later, the ground of the moor is composed largely of peat, a porous material made up of thousands of years' dead vegetation which never decomposed. The rain which fell here was absorbed and held in this dense material, which made walking on it like treading on a sponge. Numerous streams and rivers run through the moor and I found myself stepping over and in some cases into them in order to make my way up the slope.

FIGURE 67 *A Dartmoor stream*

FIGURE 68 *Granite rocks on the summit of a Dartmoor tor*

The tor itself was farther away than I had guessed. The lack of trees made distances difficult to gauge, and the better part of an hour went by before I approached the summit. The closer I came to the top, the more rocks there were, and it was with some relief that I finally arrived at the weathered rock formation at the crown of the hill.

The grey rocks towering above my head were smoothed by wind and rain. I scrambled among the nooks and crannies and imagined what sorts of magical creatures might make their home in the dark recesses. Like the town of Ottery St Mary, the moors are supposedly infested with Pixies, which are called Piskies here on the moor. They love to cause havoc in the villages on Dartmoor and are a never-ending source of trouble. I had also heard legends of a dragon living on the south edge of the moor among the ruins of ancient stone houses. I could easily picture it, possibly a Welsh Green as described in *Fantastic Beasts and Where to Find Them*. From this height, a dragon would have been able to spot prey and swoop down for the kill. I didn't see any likely victims from my vantage point atop

FIGURE 69 *Dartmoor tors*

the rocky tor, but I had seen plenty of tasty sheep on the drive up onto the moor. A dragon would do quite well for himself up here.

I was most interested, though, in Quidditch. As I gazed around me at the wide expanses, I could see that this would be a perfect place to hide a Quidditch pitch. Great smooth areas of moorland spread out below me, with tors all around to hide any Quidditch goings-on. The whole purpose of playing in such a remote location was to keep the matches a secret from the Muggles, after all.

According to the books, the Wizards' Council made a law back in 1326 that no Quidditch matches were to be played within fifty miles of a Muggle town. That rule would be almost impossible to follow in Britain as there are villages everywhere. Eventually the Wizards' Council members were so fed up with the lack of caution among witches and wizards that they wrote a famous amendment to their law which stated that Quidditch was outlawed 'anywhere near any place where there is the slightest chance that a Muggle might be watching or we'll see how well you can play whilst chained

FIGURE 70 *Wild Dartmoor ponies*

to a dungeon wall' (*Quidditch Through the Ages*, chapter 5). On the moors, at least, the few Muggles living nearby could be bewitched not to notice and the hills would hide the game from anyone else wandering by. I didn't see any evidence of a Quidditch pitch as I gazed around over miles of moorland. The Council's threat must have been taken to heart.

The ramble down the tor was a lot quicker than the climb to the top. I got back to my car and drove on, at one point passing a small herd of wild Dartmoor ponies drinking from one of the innumerable pools of water near the road. I stopped and took some pictures. They were completely unafraid of me, grazing all around me as I walked onto a low rise nearby. From this vantage point, I saw spread out below me the green Devon countryside with its hedgerows and fields. The view was stunning, on one side wild, windswept moorland with shaggy ponies drinking at a pool, and on the other a breathtaking vista of green farms and scattered villages. No wonder Rowling considered this part of England to be magical.

QUIDDITCH STADIUMS ON THE MOORS

As it became more difficult to hide Quidditch matches from the Muggles, the Department of Magical Games and Sports, which is part of the Ministry of Magic, disbanded many of the teams and established the British and Irish League in 1674. Teams in Britain do not have their own home fields for matches; instead, Quidditch stadiums have been erected on a number of deserted moors. Players and fans come from all over Britain to attend these matches. Various charms and magical effects have been used to prevent Muggles from accidentally discovering these stadiums.

✦ Bodmin Moor

This moor was the location of the famous match of 1884 in which a Snitch escaped after eluding capture by the Seekers for six months of play. The Snitch is said to be living wild on the moor still.

Bodmin Moor is located in eastern Cornwall, near Devon. All of the land is privately owned; one might guess that the area used for the Quidditch pitch is on the property of a witch or wizard. Bodmin Moor, like many moors, is the home of many legends, including one of a strange creature, the Beast of Bodmin, living wild on the moor. Perhaps this is the source of Rowling's idea of an escaped wild Snitch.

✦ Exmoor

Exmoor National Park is the home of a new Quidditch stadium, which was originally covered with an Invisibility Charm (spectators were advised to collect Re-Visibility Spectacles from the ticket sellers so they would be able to see the stadium and the match). Things didn't work out very well with the Invisibility Charm, however, and fans complained that they couldn't see their seats, let alone the match. As a result, the charm has since been lifted, with plans to instead try a special "Ministry of Magic Fog".

Exmoor is a vast area of moorland in central and north Devon.

✦ Ellis Moor

As happens on occasion, a recent match here had to be relocated when Muggles were camping near the stadium.

The location of Ellis Moor is unknown.

✦ Ilkley Moor

This stadium recently hosted a match between Puddlemere United and the Holyhead Harpies. Bad feeling between the two teams threatened to result in violence and the Ministry of Magic took the unusual step of confiscating fans' wands at the gate, though according to *Quidditch Through the Ages*, this was actually a violation of the spectators' civil rights.

Ilkley Moor is an expanse of moorland above the town of Ilkley in West Yorkshire.

✦ Quidditch World Cup Stadium

Built on a deserted moor, the actual location of which is unknown, for the World Cup in 1994. Several large campsites existed around the area, run by Muggles, and the witches and wizards who came to see the match set up their magical tents there. The Muggles who ran the campsites had to be dosed with spells to prevent them seeing all the magical goings-on.

✦ Yorkshire Moors

Fans were advised to cheer quietly here because Muggles occasionally come looking for the source of the all the noise.

A steam railway crosses the North Yorkshire Moors, and along that line you will find the station at Goathland which doubled for Hogsmeade Station in the first two films. North York Moors National Park is in eastern Yorkshire, bordering on the North Sea.

SOURCE: the Harry Potter books and the Daily Prophet newsletters

I drove on down a small road called B3212. I was grateful that it was daylight, not only because I could see the glorious landscapes around me but also because I had heard about a truly frightening ghost which is reported to wander this road at night. Drivers have told of suddenly seeing a pair of disembodied hairy hands gripping their steering wheels or the handlebars of their bicycles or motorcycles, which steer them off the road to crash. I had no desire to see any such thing.

I had heard other tales of the moor that interested me, for instance that witches had lived here, and many of them could change into the shape of animals. If these were witches from the Harry Potter books, they would be called Animagi. One witch in particular, who went by the name Old Moll, could turn herself into a large hare and was fond of doing so to lead the local huntsmen and their hounds on a merry chase through the moors. I couldn't help compare Old Moll's story to that of Wendelin the Weird, who we are told in book three used to allow herself to be caught and burned at the stake for a thrill. She would cast a Flame Freezing Charm to protect herself from the flames, then scream and carry on convincingly. Old Moll, I guessed, had a similar sense of humour.

Further up on the moor, I came to the town of Princetown, which is dominated by the grey and forbidding Dartmoor Prison. This prison is reputed to be escape-proof, but even if you do escape, you'll end up lost on the moors and probably die of exposure or be eaten by the dragons. I chose a more hospitable destination in town, however. The Old Police Station Café offered Devon cream tea, traditionally served with scones, strawberry jam, and clotted cream. Devon clotted cream is reputed to be the best in England (although folks in Cornwall will argue that theirs is superior) and since legend tells that clotted cream was a gift from the piskies of the moor, I had to try it. The jam was only passable, arriving at my table pre-packaged in plastic, but the clotted cream made up for it. I was tempted to lick every bit out of the stoneware pot it was served in.

I left Princetown stuffed with scones and clotted cream and made my way back to the west and down from the moor through Tavistock. Night falls early in November, and I wanted to get to my next destination before dark: Godric's Hollow, the ancestral home of the Potter family.

✦ Godric's Hollow ✦

What had been a sunny morning on the moor became a rainy afternoon in North Devon. I was heading for the little village of Shebbear, thanks to the excellent work done by John Kearns, who is one of the staff of the Harry Potter Lexicon website. John painstakingly gathered clues from the books and then searched maps of the West Country and combed the countryside using Google Earth, looking for a village that fitted the description. Shebbear, John discovered, seemed to have all the required features of the Godric's Hollow from the books. Sure, quite a few villages have a war memorial, a church with a graveyard, a post office and a pub; but what made Shebbear the only likely candidate, from what John could tell, was that the arrangement of these features around a small square makes sense with the sequence of events in the story.

John and I talked excitedly about what he had discovered. Had he really found a village which matched the Godric's Hollow in the books? We wondered what the village was actually like. After all, there's only so much you can learn from old photographs online and from spying on places with Google Earth. For all we knew, Shebbear could be grey and charmless, hardly a place where one could find a sense of wonder and magic. Now that I was here in Britain, I just had to visit the town and see. So I set my GPS for Shebbear and drove back into the single-track lanes of Devon, this time passing over the A30 at Okehampton and heading northwest.

The drive took me from motorway to two-lane roads to more of the sort of narrow lanes meandering through fields and hedgerows that I'd encountered around Ottery St Mary. This time I wasn't just wandering blindly; I knew where I was going. But what would I find there? Would the village be isolated enough or have the sort of feeling to it that I was looking for? Would I be able to imagine a magical cottage just outside of the village, set apart enough that no one would have noticed it for years? The cottage that Harry's parents lived and died in was such a place, abandoned and forgotten by the Muggles who lived nearby. Would I find somewhere like that in this small Devon farm village?

FIGURE 71   *A Devon lane*

Signposts where the lanes intersected pointed me towards the town. On either side, the tangled, impenetrable hedgerows obscured the farm buildings and houses. The rain ended and I got out to take a picture or two near one of the wooden signposts. I looked at it closely. The mileage numbers didn't make sense. I was sure that the sign I passed five minutes ago had said that Shebbear was two miles off, but after twisting and turning around following my GPS instructions, I found I hadn't made any progress: the sign I was looking at also said that Shebbear was two miles away. Was this an example of a Muggle-Repelling charm at work, so that I would wander lost until I remembered that I had somewhere else to be and never arrived in Shebbear at all? If this was the moor, I might suspect piskies at work. I angled for a picture of a tree against the rainclouds and realised that there was a bit of a rainbow visible just beneath its branches. I was still outside the town, among questionable signposts in a maze of hedgerows, but I took the rainbow as a good sign. I drove on.

Without any warning, I was in the village. After squeezing past a large truck that filled up the entire road, I rolled into the village square and looked around to get my bearings. The Norman church stood tall and square on my left, and I could see the rows of gravestones beyond the lychgate. Just down the lane to the right I spotted the post office. Across the square I saw the Devil's Stone Inn, where I hoped to secure a room for the night. The buildings around the square were hundreds of years old at least. Lanes led off in several directions. So far so good! I couldn't wait to explore.

I wanted to match up the storyline in the book to the arrangement of buildings and roads. Harry and Hermione had Apparated to the edge of town under an Invisibility Cloak, and then walked into the square past the pub. I walked away from my car and stood in the middle of the square facing the Devil's Stone Inn. I glanced to my right: they must have come down that narrow lane there in order to pass this pub on their way to the church. I walked down that road a short way and turned back, looking toward the square from the same direction Harry and Hermione would have looked as they entered the town.

FIGURE 72 *The village square in Shebbear*

FIGURE 73 *The pub is on the right, so this is the way Harry and Hermione would have entered the square*

The pub was now on my right as I walked into the square. The church ahead of me was set back from the road. A couple of buildings stood in front of it, but just to the left of them was an archway with a gate into the churchyard beyond. A gnarled and twisted old oak tree stood on a small lawn by the gate, and next to the tree sat a large rock. From what I could tell, the rock had been recently moved – a rock-shaped patch of bare earth marred the grass just next to it. I had heard of this rock, called the Devil's Stone, and would find out its full story later. For now, I wanted to look around the graveyard.

Harry and Hermione had visited the Godric's Hollow graveyard on Christmas Eve, looking for the graves of his parents, Lily and James. The book describes the snowy ground smattered with colour from the stained glass windows of the church. As I approached the gate, I was pleased to see that the church in Shebbear had lovely stained glass windows facing the rows and rows of gravestones.

I opened the gate – not a kissing gate as described in the books, which would typically be found between pastures or fields, but a wooden gate under a small roof. From there I wandered along row after row of headstones, looking at inscriptions. I didn't see any names

FIGURE 74   *The gate into the Shebbear churchyard*

FIGURE 75   *The churchyard in Shebbear*

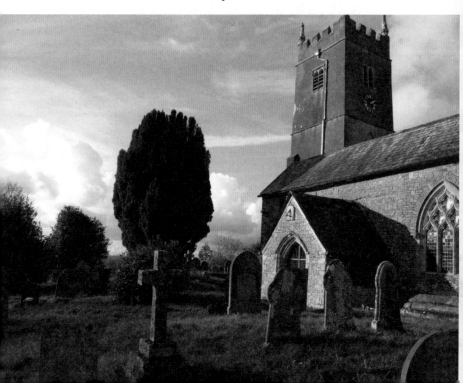

of wizard families from the books, of course, but I wasn't surprised. At the bottom of the hill, a row of trees marked the far end of the churchyard, so I turned right and walked along, glancing back up towards the church and imagining Harry and Hermione doing the same on a snowy December night. I wasn't sure what I was looking for, but I kept walking and gazing at the old weathered stones.

At the end of one of the rows, just where the trees hung over from the hedge, I saw the name Lily on an old headstone mottled with lichen. I looked a little closer. She had been married to someone named James. I stood and stared. Lily and James.

FIGURE 76 *A surprising headstone*

Their surname wasn't Potter, and James was the second name of the man, not the first, but still…seeing the names James and Lily together on the headstone in this out of the way village churchyard in Devon was astonishing. The inscription on the stone was from the Book of Common Prayer: "In the midst of life we are in death." That wasn't quite the quotation from the books, but it had the same ring to it. I knew that Godric's Hollow existed only in the pages of the Harry Potter books, but it was nonetheless tremendously exciting to see those names on a grave in a small Devon village churchyard.

I found my way back out of the hilly churchyard, through the gate, past the oak tree and the ancient stone, and back into the square. In front of me now was the war memorial. The book's version is a tall obelisk, while the one here in Shebbear is a smaller stone with names engraved on it. I knew it was too much to expect that the memorial would magically change to show the stone images of the Potter family, but I kept looking at it anyway. Everything was so close to the descriptions in the book, I half believed that if I just looked intently enough, I would see the stone transform.

I opened the door to the Devil's Stone Inn and made my way into the bar. A large dog sniffed at me and wagged his tail while the landlady told me that yes, of course I could have a room for the night. In fact, I was the only guest. I ordered a small lunch and a cup of tea, then followed her up to the first floor and down the hall to drop off my bags. The room was small, of course, but completely charming, and she handed me two keys, one for the room and the other for the front door of the inn. They'd all be leaving for the afternoon, she told me, and wouldn't be back until the restaurant opened for dinner around six. I went back down to collect my lunch and asked the young woman behind the bar if she had any information about the Inn. Did I know, she asked me, that The Devil's Stone Inn is reputed

FIGURE 77 *The Shebbear churchyard*

to be the most haunted pub in England? She passed me a folder with information about all the ghostly sightings in the building, which I read through with interest, then thanked her with a brave smile and carried my lunch tray back upstairs. A little while later I heard the front door of the inn close solidly and all was silent.

I ate my lunch of bread, meat and cheese and sipped my tea, then tried to write about my experience in Shebbear so far. I found it hard to describe the feeling. I know that Godric's Hollow is a fictional place, and I'm quite sure that Rowling didn't visit here and borrow her impressions and memories of Shebbear when she was writing. Even so, I found myself enchanted by the charm of this little town, the kind of magic that comes from the quiet beauty of an ancient farm village lost among the lanes and fields of North Devon. The whole village seems to resonate with history. Shebbear was mentioned in the Doomsday Book, the register of lands and holding commissioned in 1086 by William I. The church was built in the 11th century and consecrated St Michael's in 1358.

As I wrote, the church bells began to ring. It was just a little before four in the afternoon, but already it was getting dark on this late November day. A white bus rumbled to a stop outside in the square and a group of children disembarked, bundled against the autumn chill in jumpers and coats over their school uniforms. They scattered down the lanes to my left and right, heading home. I watched them go by and wondered if they'd read the Harry Potter books, and if they had any idea that their little village in the north of Devon bore an uncanny resemblance to the home town of Harry's parents, the place where Albus Dumbledore's mother and sister lay buried, a place where wizard families would be living unnoticed all around them.

I heard sounds from the pub below and thought first that my hosts had returned. On the other hand, it was a bit early for dinner. Was someone else about in the inn? Then I shivered a little, remembering the conversation with the woman at the bar and what I'd read about ghosts in the corridors and on the stairs. I knew that the room I was staying in, number six, wasn't the one where most of the haunted events were witnessed, but even so I was just a bit on edge. I gathered my courage and stepped out onto the landing. All was quiet again.

I headed down the stairs, not listening for the sound of a giggling child ghost in the hall or footsteps following me, and stepped out of the front door, locking it behind me. I walked with as much casual ease as I could muster across the square.

I had emailed a few people in Shebbear before I came and in one exchange had promised to have a cup of tea with Paul, an affable man who lives on the square near the Inn. I tapped on his door and he greeted me warmly, showed me into his kitchen, and set about making tea.

While he put the kettle on, Paul told me about his house, which as far as he could tell was built in the 1600s. He and his wife are working on the building, trying to preserve some of the centuries-old charm while doing some remodelling. The walls are constructed from cob, a mixture of clay, sand, and straw that is similar to adobe, and he showed me a place where he'd done some work so I could see the rough clay exposed. Hundreds of years ago the cob was often mixed with manure from the farm animals, and when Paul was restoring his house, he could occasionally catch a whiff of the earthy, animal smell from centuries before. Inside one of the walls, Paul had found a witch jar, or what was left of one: a witch jar is a small glass or pottery vessel filled with nails, needles, and other small

FIGURE 78 *After the rain in Shebbear*

items placed inside the wall of a house to protect the inhabitants from witches.

I figured Paul would be a good person to ask about the stone I'd seen on the lawn by the church. We settled down with our tea and he explained about the Turning of the Stone. No one is quite sure where the tradition originated, he told me, although there are plenty of interesting theories. The stone in question is a large chunk of granite which geologists say is not of local origin. Legends suggest that the stone fell from the Devil's pocket when he was cast out of heaven, or that it was an ancient pagan altar. One particularly fascinating tale suggests that the stone was originally quarried to be the foundation stone for a nearby church, but that the stone mysteriously vanished

FIGURE 79 *The Devil's Stone*

from that location and appeared in Shebbear. Every time the stone was returned to the church it reappeared in its current location, presumably at the hand of the Devil. Regardless of the reasons, the 'Devil's Stone' is now a permanent feature of the village square.

Every fifth of November, Paul told me, the villagers gather for the Turning of the Stone. The ceremony begins with the wild ringing of the bells of St Michael's church, presumably to scare the Devil away or perhaps to confuse him prior to his stone being moved, I'm not sure which. Then the bell-ringers come out onto the lawn and use poles and crowbars to pry the one-tonne stone up from the spot it has occupied for the last year. When they manage to roll it over, the town is assured of another year of good fortune. Some say that the Devil gets confused by the moving of 'his' stone and therefore can't figure out where he is when he comes to Shebbear. Others have suggested that the Devil is actually trapped under the stone and moving it baffles him enough to keep him trapped for another twelve months. A few years back, according to Paul, when the stone was rolled over, a toad hopped out from beneath it. Ancient witches believed the Devil could manifest himself as a toad, so one can only imagine the surprise when this poor toad happened to hide under that particular stone on that particular day.

I listened to the stories with fascination. Paul told me that during the World Wars, the supply of men capable of this heavy lifting was limited and one year the stone wasn't moved on November 5. Several days later folks in the village realised that they hadn't turned the stone on schedule, so quickly gathered as many people as they could and set to, with the result that the stone was finally moved, much to everyone's relief. I realised as I chatted with Paul that I had discovered another place besides Ottery St Mary which I want to visit on the fifth of November.

I thanked Paul for the tea and stories and crossed the dark square. The Devil's Stone Inn's dining room was warm and inviting, with a surprisingly good menu. After a nice dinner, I decide to go back out and see the town by moonlight. The night was rainy and cold, but I wandered outside and looked up at the square Norman-style tower of the church, outlined against the moon and clouds. I walked towards the gate into the graveyard and then over to where the Stone lay near the ancient oak tree. I thought about the thousands of years of history in this place and the traditions and stories that tied the inhabitants to their rich past. I thought about the witch jar in Paul's cob wall and the stories of ghosts haunting the Inn. Then I went back inside to sit by one of the open fireplaces in the pub, drink a pint of beer, and think how lucky I was to have found Shebbear.

The next morning the sun was shining. After a late breakfast in the pub, I explored the village a little more. Once again, I tried to orientate myself to the story in the seventh book. After Harry and Hermione had found the grave of his parents, the book says that they walked down the lane a short way and discovered the cottage in which his family had lived and died. That cottage was, according to the book, invisible to Muggles and on the other side of a gate along the road. Wouldn't it be interesting to find a gate like that, opening onto nowhere at all?

Three roads led away from the village square. The afternoon before I had worked out that Harry and Hermione would have

FIGURE 80 *One of the lanes leading away from the square*

entered the town from the post office direction in order to pass the pub on their way to the church. According to the book, after visiting the graveyard they walked down a different lane and discovered his parents' ruined cottage.

So I took the road to the left of the Inn, and found myself walking down a rather steep hill past a few houses. One building on the left caught my eye. It was fenced in and on the sky-blue gate was a sternly worded sign warning against trespassing, for the building was owned by British Telecom. That was perfectly logical, of course, but it occurred to me that if this was a magical building, I might be seeing only what a Muggle-Repelling Charm was tricking me into seeing. I decided that I wouldn't test that theory by climbing the fence, however; I had no wish to antagonise British Telecom, and could just imagine the reaction from irate BT officials if I tried to explain why I was trespassing by saying I was convinced that their telephone equipment building was in fact the magical home of Harry Potter.

FIGURE 81 *The sky-blue gate in Shebbear, with a warning sign from BT*

FIGURE 82 *A gate into an open field, with another house some way off in the distance*

At the bottom of the hill was a small crossroads with signposts pointing in different directions. To my right, however, I saw another gate. This one was set into the hedgerow along the road and, as far as I could tell, the other side was just open field. This was undoubtedly a farm gate, allowing access to the land beyond, but it made me smile. Wasn't it possible that the gate Harry and Hermione discovered would look just like that, an innocent gate that Muggles would pass off as nothing special?

In the books there is another magical house in Godric's Hollow, that of the famous magical historian Bathilda Bagshot. Harry and Hermione barely escape with their lives from the upstairs bedroom of this house when the evil Lord Voldemort and his huge snake Nagini attack them. I didn't know where to look for this house, except that it wasn't on the same road as the Potter house. So I climbed the hill back to the village square and followed the other road, down the side street towards the post office.

I wasn't really sure whether Bathilda Bagshot's house was invisible like the Potters' had been, so I looked for anything that caught my eye. There were plenty of houses and cottages lining the road.

FIGURE 83 *Another street in Shebbear*

Immediately past the square I discovered several new gates leading nowhere in particular. One was similar to the one I had seen down the hill. Another was actually an oddly mismatched section of the wall enclosing an empty plot. It wasn't really a gate at all, but I could imagine that I was being kept from seeing what it really was by magic. Maybe Bathilda's house was on the other side of one of these gates. Who could tell?

After a few more hours wandering around the town and taking pictures, I started the long drive back to London. It had been quite a trip: the Burrow, Ottery St Mary, the moors, and now Shebbear… or should I say Godric's Hollow? I started thinking about where I might go next. It was hard to imagine ever being able to match the success of this expedition.

MAGICAL CREATURES
IN THE WEST COUNTRY

The West Country is home not only to witches and wizards but also to a number of magical creatures. While some creatures are found all over Britain, a few are native to these counties in particular.

Bowtruckle These tiny creatures, which appear to be 'made of twigs', guard trees which are particularly useful for making wands.

Pixies Small blue creatures which love to make mischief, pixies prefer to live near towns where they can cause the most trouble. Pixies are part of the folklore of many areas of the West Country, especially Cornwall, and Dartmoor in particular seems to be overflowing with them; Ottery St Mary commemorates a day hundreds of years ago when the pesky little creatures were banished from their town.

Porlock Dorset is the home of the Porlock, a shy creature covered in fur with cloven hoofs. Porlocks are 'horse guardians' and often live in the straw of stables, although you'll be lucky to see one because they are extremely shy.

Snidget This endangered species of small round bird was hunted almost to extinction after capturing one was added to the game of Quidditch in 1269. The invention of the Golden Snitch to replace it saved the little bird, but it is still endangered. The Modesty Rabnott Snidget Reservation is in Somerset.

4
THE NORTH OF ENGLAND

I said before that pretty much everything in the Harry Potter books can be seen as taking place in one of three areas of Britain: London and its environs, the West Country, and Scotland. However, there are two important events which can't be nailed down quite so exactly, both of which were very likely set somewhere in the north of England.

One of the places I wanted to find was Little Hangleton. Harry visits there against his will towards the end of book four when he is transported by Portkey to a graveyard in that small town. There he witnesses the rebirth of Lord Voldemort in a horrible Dark Magic ceremony.

The other story location I sought was a small unnamed mill town, where Severus Snape spent his unhappy childhood and befriended Lily Evans, who grew up to be Harry's mother.

Neither of these towns can be as easily pinpointed as places like Ottery St Catchpole or Charing Cross Road. I spent some time looking at maps of the north of England and considering the clues in the books, which are ambiguous at best. But I decided just to give it a shot and see what I could turn up.

✦

✦ Little Hangleton ✦

The village of Little Hangleton is the original home of Voldemort's mother and father. His mother, Merope Gaunt, was a witch, while his father, Tom Riddle, was a Muggle. In the book, we see the Gaunts living in a hovel near the village; they are illiterate and crude, existing in filth and ruin, speaking the language of snakes to each other. At the time of Voldemort's birth in the early 1900s, the Gaunts were the last remaining remnant of the pureblood line of Salazar Slytherin himself. Marvolo Gaunt, the patriarch of the clan, held fast to his pureblood status and to a few relics of his ancestors: a ring with a strange symbol on it and a locket which had belonged to Slytherin. His son Morfin was a degenerate and his daughter, Merope, was abused.

The Riddle family, on the other hand, was rich and arrogant. Merope fell in love with Tom Riddle and bewitched him to marry her. Merope became pregant, but Tom Riddle deserted her, leaving her to give birth to the child in a London orphanage, where she died a short time later. The child, also named Tom Riddle, turned up in Little Hangleton one summer night sixteen years later and killed his father and grandparents in their manor house on the hill overlooking Little Hangleton.

The books give us very few clues to identify Little Hangleton. One detail is somewhat helpful, however. In the fourth book we read about another murder performed by Tom Riddle, many years after he killed his father and grandparents. Now known as Lord Voldemort, he took up residence in the decaying manor house in Little Hangleton. When the caretaker came poking around to investigate the intruders, Voldemort killed him, at which point, according to the book, Harry Potter woke up with his scar hurting 'two hundred miles away'.

I drew a circle on a map of Britain, centred on the northern part of Surrey, with a radius of two hundred miles, and looked carefully at the places where it crossed land: Cornwall and Yorkshire. Little Hangleton must be in one of those two areas.

I did a Google search and discovered to my surprise that Hangleton is a real place. Could it be that easy? Of course not: Hangleton turned

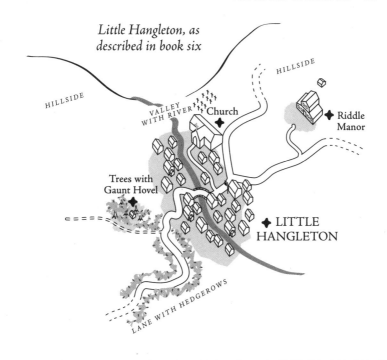

Little Hangleton, as described in book six

HILLSIDE

HILLSIDE

VALLEY WITH RIVER

Church

Riddle Manor

Trees with Gaunt Hovel

✦ LITTLE HANGLETON

LANE WITH HEDGEROWS

NOT-SO-MAGICAL PLACE

Little Hangleton

Location: About two hundred miles from Little Whinging, which places it either in Yorkshire or the western part of Cornwall.

Function: The village where Voldemort's mother, a witch named Merope Gaunt, and his father, a rich Muggle named Tom Riddle, lived.

How to get there: Harry is taken to the graveyard there by a Portkey.

Description: The village is in a valley. A churchyard in the village is the location of the graves of the Riddles, Voldemort's father and grandparents. The Riddle manor house stands on a hillside overlooking the town. On the opposite hillside, hidden in trees, is the Gaunt family hovel.

Additional details: The road leading into the village past the Gaunt house is surrounded by hedgerows.

out to be not a town but a housing estate in Hove, on the outskirts of Brighton on the East Sussex coast. True, there's a fascinating old manor house dating from the fourteenth century in Hangleton, but that doesn't help. This Hangleton is less than fifty miles from the area of Surrey near Berkshire where Harry was probably sleeping. The geography just doesn't fit.

What I needed to find was a small town in a valley with a church and a prominent manor house outside of town. The road leading into the town needed to be lined at least in part with hedgerows. Simple, right?

No, not simple at all. There are plenty of place in the Yorkshire Dales which might qualify. One town that caught my eye as I pored over the map was Ingleton, in the southern part of the Yorkshire Dales. The name certainly reminded me of Hangleton, and there are a few hedgerows in the area. I studied the maps and then researched online. Ingleton was a very interesting possibility, but unfortunately I couldn't see any large manor houses which would be visible on a hill overlooking the town. Could Ingleton be Hangleton? Maybe. But so could any number of other towns on the map. I spotted quite a few old houses near some of the towns, but were they on hillsides? I could hardly visit every town in Yorkshire, hoping for a match.

I also examined maps of Cornwall where the two-hundred-mile line crosses. The landscape is very interesting in that area because of the many china clay pits, but it was impossible to locate only one town that would be a perfect match for Little Hangleton.

So I was left with a quandary. North or west? I was tempted to decide upon Yorkshire because of the valleys and hills, but Cornwall certainly isn't flat. In the end, I had to give up. Little Hangleton remains elusive; there are just too many possibilities. Perhaps an extra clue will come my way at some point and I'll be off on the train to see if I can find the Riddle House on a hill overlooking a small village in a valley.

✦ Spinner's End ✦

Severus Snape lived his unhappy childhood in an unnamed village, in a small terraced house on a cobbled street called Spinner's End, near a river. As a boy Severus befriended a girl who lived nearby, Lily Evans, with whom he shared his pain at living with an angry, violent father, a Muggle named Tobias Snape. Severus's mother Eileen was a witch, and since he had inherited her magic, he looked forward desperately to leaving his miserable home and attending Hogwarts. Years later, the adult Severus still lived in this small house on Spinner's End.

There is an actual street called Spinner's End Drive in Cradley Heath, a suburb of Birmingham; however that particular Spinner's End, located just off the High Street, doesn't fit the description in the book at all. The houses there are very new, all built in the identical artfully quaint style – a far cry from the broken-down workers' terraces mentioned in the books. Cradley Heath, furthermore, is located nowhere near a river.

There's another Spinner's End in Weston-super-Mare in Avon, near Bristol. It is located near a river, but it's part of a very modern suburb, a lot more like Little Whinging than the depressed town in the books.

I found quite a few clues to help me as I searched for Spinner's End. In book six, Narcissa and Bellatrix arrive in the town on a path alongside a dirty, smelly river, scramble up the bank, past a railing, and across a cobbled street. The houses near and along Spinner's End are brick and in straight rows, most likely the kind of small terraces built in the nineteenth century for workers at the mills. The books tell us that many of the houses on Spinner's End are boarded up, which suggests that the area is quite run-down; some of the street-lights are broken as well. In an excellent essay on the Harry Potter Lexicon website, Claire M. Jordan describes houses of this kind. Many would be joined to the adjacent houses back to back as well as side to side, with two rooms on each floor. They would often have only outdoor lavatory facilities and no running water. This might explain why Snape never seemed to learn the habit of regular washing.

FIGURE 84 *Spinner's End in Cradley Heath near Birmingham*

NOT-SO-MAGICAL PLACE

Spinner's End

Location: Spinner's End is a cobbled street near a dirty river, in a mill town with a chimney looming overhead.

Function: At the end of this street is the childhood home of Severus Snape.

How to get there: It's a Muggle street and a Muggle house, so no magic is required to visit. Bellatrix and Narcissa Apparate to a rubbish-strewn path next to the river, scramble up the bank and walk down a few cobbled streets to find the house.

Description (the house): Snape's home is a small terraced house in a run-down part of town, with broken street-lights and the windows of some houses boarded up.

Additional details: The front door of the house opens right onto the street.

Finding the fictional Spinner's End would be tricky, even with all those clues. Towns with mills and terraced workers' houses can be found all over Britain, particularly in the north of England. If the name "Spinner's End" is any clue, the town where Snape grew up might have had a textile mill, and the book mentions a tall chimney looming over the town. The city of Manchester was once known as the "town of tall chimneys" because so many textile mills were to be found there. Yorkshire and Scotland also had many such mills. That left me with a lot of places to look.

All the old mills in Britain are closed now. Many are derelict or have been torn down. A few have been preserved as museums, such as the Queen Street Mill in Lancashire, billed as the "world's only surviving 19th century steam-powered weaving mill". Many of the tall chimneys still stand, thankfully without the plumes of black coal smoke which polluted cities and countryside in years past. Would it be possible to find a place which matched all the clues to Spinner's End? Would there be a dirty river, cobbled streets, and rows of 200-year-old two-up two-down workers' houses? Where would I begin to look for a place like that?

In her essay, Jordan argues persuasively that the town is located in the area around Manchester. The cities and towns in this area certainly have a heritage of mills and factories and many of them could stand in for the town in the book. Cities in this area inspired Charles Dickens's fictional mill town of Coketown in the novel *Hard Times*. (The dreary town of Cokeworth mentioned in the first Harry Potter book may have been named after Dickens's 'Coketown'.) Dickens's depiction of Coketown is very similar to how Rowling describes the area around Spinner's End:

> It was a town of red brick, or of brick that would have been red if the smoke and ashes had allowed it; but as matters stood, it was a town of unnatural red and black like the painted face of a savage. It was a town of machinery and tall chimneys, out of which interminable serpents of smoke trailed themselves for ever and ever, and never got uncoiled. It had a black canal in it, and a river that ran purple with ill-smelling dye, and vast piles of building full of windows where there was a rattling and a trembling all day long, and where the piston of the steam-engine worked monotonously up and down,

like the head of an elephant in a state of melancholy madness. It
contained several large streets all very like one another, and many
small streets still more like one another, inhabited by people equally
like one another, who all went in and out at the same hours, with
the same sound upon the same pavements, to do the same work,
and to whom every day was the same as yesterday and tomorrow,
and every year the counterpart of the last and the next.

(*Hard Times*, BOOK I, CHAPTER 5)

Jordan suggests several potential locations for Spinner's End outside
of the large city of Manchester itself. The small town of New Mills
is one such possibility, located along several rivers and home to a
number of old textile mills. As with other such towns, many of the
older working-class terraces have been demolished; but the remains
of the mills still stand along the river, and perhaps I could find some
hint of Spinner's End in the historic areas of the town. If nothing
else, I'd get a sense of what the industrial north of England was like.
So one grey, rainy Saturday in January I took the train north from
London's St Pancras station. I changed trains at Sheffield and took a
two-carriage local that stopped at small stations through the beautiful
Hope Valley. As I approached New Mills, the train windows revealed
mountains and valleys, tumbling streams and farms. Tall chimneys
rose above many of the towns, but these places still had the kind of
rural charm that I had discovered and loved in the West Country.

FIGURE 85   *New Mills Central station*

While the fields in Devon were separated by hedgerows, however, here in the north the fields were laced with stone walls.

The station at New Mills was built from local sandstone in the late 1800s, when this town was in its industrial heyday. Just beyond the platform, two tunnels carried the tracks into the mountainside, running for all I could tell under the town itself. I walked up the station road and found myself at the top of a long path down a steep hill, surrounded by peaceful woods; at the bottom a river ran fast and furious, the water the colour of hot chocolate. I walked down the hill towards it, wondering if this could fit the description in the books. I couldn't imagine Narcissa and Bellatrix appearing on that riverbank. The scramble to the top would be an eighty-feet vertical climb. And there were no chimneys to be seen.

I followed the path by the river. Around a bend I spotted a group of huge brick structures. They were in pretty bad shape; many of the windows were broken and some of the walls had partially collapsed. Ahead of me a sign indicated the Millennium Walkway, which turned out to be a spectacular curved bridge that hugged the ravine wall and took me past the disused buildings, which a plaque on the walkway identified as a former mill. Below me the river roared over weirs. To be honest, it was a little unnerving to walk above that raging water.

FIGURE 86 & 87 *Walking along the river gorge in New Mills, among the ruins of nineteenth-century mills.*

So far I couldn't see this river as similar to the description in the books. I was at the bottom of a gorge surrounded by the ruins of century-old mills. The river didn't look like the one described in the book at all, and no one would climb up to the town from here, not when they could have Apparated closer to their destination. I passed more remains of brick buildings and a chimney or two, but those didn't fit either: the chimneys would barely reach the top of the cliffs, not loom over the town. I kept walking and looking for the pathway to New Mills itself and soon spotted a sign which pointed to the town centre, indicating a steep trail upwards.

It was a long trek up the hillside. Once at the top, I walked up the road and into the town itself. In spite of the mist and rain, the street of shops I encountered was pleasant and inviting. I noticed not one but two fish and chip shops quite near the place where I'd climbed up from the river. In the book, a fox had been nosing at a fish and chip wrapper near where Narcissa and Bellatrix had appeared. That didn't say much, of course, since every town has fish and chip shops, but I was encouraged to see them. I continued towards the centre of the town.

What I was hoping to find were dingy old terraced houses of the sort described in the books, the kind of house where Snape might live. While plenty of the buildings in New Mills were quite old and some were the right style, none that I had seen so far were dilapidated or disused. I was also hoping to see a tall chimney poking into the sky over the town – I had seen such chimneys in other villages as I passed them on the train. Several were simple and straight, while others flared at the top with fanciful constructions of brickwork; bricklayers often added these kinds of decorations to the tops of the chimneys they were constructing because they were paid by the brick. Unfortunately, all the chimneys I'd seen so far in New Mills had been at the bottom of the river gorge.

However, as I followed the street around and crossed the Union Road bridge, my luck changed. A tall chimney rose in the distance. The houses along the road were exactly the type described in the books, although they were not in particularly poor condition. I took a side street and cut through a few alleys, where I saw the right kind of arrangement of houses and chimney; but I wasn't satisfied. The river was much too far away and far below.

FIGURE 88 *A chimney rises above New Mills*

I walked on, now off the main street, heading more or less towards the chimney. At the end of a small industrial roadway I climbed a few stone steps tucked among some bushes, and what I discovered was a complete surprise: instead of another road, I found myself at the edge of a canal. Colourful canal boats were moored on the far bank. The chimney now rose quite close, just along the canal on the other side of the bridge I could see a few hundred feet away. I stopped and thought about the description in the sixth book. Could the dirty river have actually been a canal? I couldn't think of any reason why not. Here was a flat pathway which was even cobbled in spots, and plenty of bushes and undergrowth to hide a fox. Assorted rubbish was tangled in the weeds and floating in the canal. I saw a McDonald's soft drink cup and Mars Bar wrapper, but the closest

FIGURE 89
(right) Back alleys
in New Mills

FIGURE 90
Workers' cottages

I could come to a fish and chip wrapper was a dead carp bobbing along the edge of the canal.

I started walking down the towpath, watching where I put my feet because the path was apparently very popular with dogs. The path was cobbled in places, stones and mud in others. A canal boat puttered past, its skipper huddled under an umbrella. As I passed under the bridge, I noticed an odd, sickly sweet smell. It wasn't coming from the canal but from the factories to my right. Across the water a steep embankment led up to more houses. I walked as far as a bend in the waterway where the landscape changed to woods and fields, then made my way back. When I found the steps again and scrambled down to the road, I noticed something I hadn't seen before. Angling from the end of that street was another, Woodside Street, lined with rows of small two-up two-down houses.

I looked up at the fronts of the houses. No one could call them derelict or disused; as far as I could tell they were well-kept and tidy, with hanging baskets outside the doors and welcome mats. The

FIGURE 91 *The canal and the path*

FIGURE 92
Victorian terraces near
the canal in New Mills

FIGURE 93 *The path near the River Sett, litter and all*

doors opened directly onto the narrow pavement. I stopped and chatted with an elderly resident and asked him the age of his house. Older than he was, he responded with a laugh, and then guessed that it would have been built in the 1800s as worker housing. I thanked him and wandered on.

Could this be Spinner's End? Would Snape's house be on a street like this, of old houses near a canal?

To learn more about the history of a mill town of this sort, I visited the town's Heritage Centre, a museum housed in an old brick building along the top of the river gorge. Inside I found a lot of information about the town and the surrounding area, including a number of excellent displays; I particularly enjoyed the crawl-through coal-mine tunnel and a glorious model of the town as it had appeared in the 1880s. I had spent enough time wandering around the town by now to be able to spot the places I'd been, reproduced on that model. From the diorama and the narration that accompanied it, I realised that I had one more place I needed to check out. New Mills, I discovered, had *two* rivers, along with the canal. The rushing river I'd seen along the Millenium Walkway was the Goyt. The other river, the Sett, connected with the Goyt near the Heritage Centre. Upstream of that point the Sett flowed past several areas which had been filled with workers' houses over a hundred years ago. I wondered if I would be able to find my Spinner's End there.

So I took the path outside the Centre which led back down into the gorge. This time I followed the Sett upstream to a bend in the river, where the buildings were a lot closer to the water. Here, just like I saw by the canal, I found a walkway along the river. I looked to my left and saw another path, leading up the embankment towards the houses. This could easily fit the description in the books, and when I climbed the hill I discovered that the street above was indeed cobbled and lined with terraces.

This was getting interesting. The street was called Meal Street and a disused chimney rose above it from the ruins of a mill near the river. Some of the houses on Meal Street were as neat and tidy as those I'd seen elsewhere in New Mills, but some were run-down with their windows painted over and rubbish scattered around. Snape's house, I knew from the books, would be located at the end of the street, so I

FIGURE 94 *Cobbled street up from the river*

walked over the cobblestones until I reached the end. The last house was an odd one, with no windows above the ground floor. The door opened right onto the street, which was paved at this point. When I looked back, I could see the chimney in the distance.

I imagined how the story would fit with what I had just discovered. Bellatrix and Narcissa would have appeared next to the river, which was littered with trash, and walked up the embankment to the end of Meal Street. Turning right, they would have walked down that road, which was mostly cobblestones, until they reached this last house. It all fitted very nicely. I wanted to corroborate one last detail, though. In book seven, Snape meets Lily on a playground. Sure enough, the New Mills Elementary School was just two streets away.

On the long train journey back to London I thought about New Mills. I had expected something different, a flat, boring expanse of derelict houses overshadowed by the harsh remains of an industrial past. I had imagined the kind of miserable environment described by

FIGURE 95 *The unusual house at the end of the street*

Dickens, and perhaps Rowling had had the same thing in mind. In years past, New Mills certainly had looked that way. Today, however, life has moved on. The old workers' houses have been renovated and in many cases replaced, and what I found now was a pleasant, even picturesque town nestled in the hills along the river. Even so, the remnants of a difficult and dreary life remain in the ruins of the mills and the cobbled lanes with rows of old houses. I realised, just as I had in Surrey, that the places in the Harry Potter books could be a lot more interesting than my stereotyped impressions. Spinner's End could be a street along a rushing river or a canal where people have lived and worked for centuries. Spinner's End, I decided, could be just like Meal Street or Woodside Street in New Mills.

5

SCOTLAND

If I was going to hide a magical castle somewhere in Britain, I would very likely choose the Scottish Highlands. You could hide just about anything there among the mountains and forests…dragons, wizarding villages, Quidditch matches, and certainly a castle.

Scotland was the third main area of Britain where the stories take place and I had a few places from the books to look for. Of course, Hogwarts was at the top of my list, along with Hogsmeade, the little village nearby. A large Kelpie lived in Loch Ness, according to *Fantastic Beasts and Where to Find Them* and also the Daily Prophet newsletters, so I had to travel there. I hoped to spot a dragon or two as well, since the Hebridean Black supposedly inhabited the higher mountain ranges of the Hebrides Islands. Finally, the infamous Isle of Drear and the wizard prison Azkaban were to be found somewhere off the northern coast.

With the exception of Loch Ness, all of these places would only appear to wizards, so I would have to use some detective work to find likely locations. I didn't mind, though: after all, how often does one have an excuse to wander around the Scottish Highlands taking pictures?

In the Highlands, mountains and forests rise above vast stretches of rolling moorland. In summer, the hills are covered with heather and wildflowers. Treacherous bogs, lochs and streams are everywhere, waiting to trap the unwary or unprepared, so the wilder stretches of Highland moor would be best viewed from the safety of the road or explored only on the footpaths that criss-cross them. The weather has a habit of changing from bright sunshine to rain squalls with barely a warning; I had heard that a warm jacket and a pair of gloves were always advisable, even in the middle of summer. Even if I couldn't find magic of the Harry Potter variety, I knew I would find plenty to enchant me in Scotland.

✦

PLACES TO FIND

Scotland

Loch Ness: The books and the Daily Prophet newsletters tell us that somewhere in this loch, one of the largest in Scotland, lives a creature which Muggles call the Loch Ness Monster. *Fantastic Beasts* identifies it as a very large Kelpie.

The Hebrides: These islands off the west coast of Scotland are home to the Hebridean Black dragon. The Pride of Portree Quidditch team hails from Skye, the largest of the Hebrides.

The Isle of Drear: Located off the northernmost tip of Scotland, this island is home to the fearsome creatures known as Quintapeds.

Azkaban: The wizard prison Azkaban is located on an island in the north of the North Sea, which would put it off the coast somewhere to the east of the mainland.

Hogsmeade: This little village is the only all-wizarding village in Britain. It's located near Hogwarts castle.

Hogwarts School of Witchcraft and Wizardry: This was the place I most hoped to find, and would be the final stop on my explorations of Harry Potter's Britain.

FIGURE 96 *Along the river in the Scottish Highlands*

FIGURE 97 *Fishing in a loch*

FIGURES 98 & 99 *The Isle of Skye*

MAGICAL ISLANDS OF SCOTLAND

Almost 800 islands lie off the coast of Scotland (including one, the Black Isle, which isn't really an island at all but a peninsula). Several of these islands appear in the Harry Potter books.

✦ The Hebrides
The Hebrides are two groups of islands, located off the west coast of the Scottish mainland. The Isle of Skye, the largest island in the Inner Hebrides, is accessible by car over the Skye Bridge at Kyle of Lochalsh. A drive through the amazing landscape of Skye takes you past dizzying cliffs overlooking the sea and up into misty mountains. Along the way you'll find ruined castles, ancient croft houses, and the charming town of Portree, where pastel-coloured buildings line the quay. The town is the home of the Pride of Portree Quidditch team. Hebridean Black dragons live in the high mountains of the Hebrides, and are traditionally cared for by the MacFusty clan of wizards.

✦ The Orkneys
The Orkney Islands, more than seventy in total although only twenty-one are inhabited, lie off the north coast of Scotland. Access to the Orkneys is by ferry from John o' Groats, a tiny village on the northernmost tip of the mainland. The Orkneys have been inhabited for thousands of years and ancient standing stone monuments abound. Somewhere among these islands, according to *Fantastic Beasts and Where to Find Them*, is the Isle of Drear. Wizarding legend tells that this island was once the home of two feuding clans, the McCliverts and the MacBoons. The feud carried on for years, culminating in the entire MacBoon clan being transfigured by the McCliverts into fearsome five-legged creatures called Quintapeds. The McClivert victory was short-lived, however: the monsters proved to be so vicious that they attacked and completely wiped out the McCliverts. Now the island and its incredibly dangerous inhabitants are magically hidden to keep unwary Muggles and wizards alike from stumbling into harm's way.

SOURCE: *Fantastic Beasts and Where to Find Them* and *Quidditch Through the Ages*

✦ Loch Ness ✦

My Scottish expedition started at Loch Ness. At more than twenty miles long and a mile wide, Loch Ness is one of the largest and deepest lochs in Scotland, and, of course, most famous for its monster. 'Nessie', as she is affectionately known, has been seen a number of times over the years, often described as having a long neck and flippers. A number of explanations have been offered for these sightings, some suggesting various animals and others pointing to wave formations or other natural phenomena. According to the Harry Potter books, though, the monster is actually a giant kelpie – a shape-shifting water horse.

On the shore stand the ruins of a castle called Urquhart (pronounced UR-kurt), which lends its name in the books to the infamous Urquhart Rackharrow. This unpleasant fellow, according

FIGURE 100 *Loch Ness in Scotland*

to the inscription on his portrait in St Mungo's seen in book five, invented something called the 'Entrail-Expelling Curse'. Urquhart Castle, or what's left of it, is quite beautiful, standing on a point overlooking the loch. When I imagine Hogwarts castle sitting on the top of a cliff overlooking a lake, I imagine Urquhart Castle. However Urquhart Castle is far too small to be Hogwarts, which is seven storeys tall, with towers rising still higher.

I drove along the north shore of Loch Ness on a beautiful sunny morning, watching for traffic on the narrow road and keeping one eye primed for any large magical reptilian creatures poking their heads above the water. The book *Fantastic Beasts and Where to Find Them* reports that the kelpie in the Loch is an ongoing problem for the Ministry of Magic because of its natural inclination to show off. Scotland, it says, has been repeatedly fined by the International Confederation of Wizards when the kelpie takes on its favourite form, that of a sea serpent, and intentionally shows itself to Muggles.

FIGURE 101 *Urquhart Castle at sunset*

FIGURE 102 *Loch Ness visitors' centre*

FIGURE 103 *The Highlands*

The Office of Misinformation at the Ministry has had its hands full making sure that all photographs of the kelpie are officially declared to be fake. The situation has really got out of hand, however: in the Daily Prophet newsletters, an article tells of the Ministry's worries about Muggles actually looking for the 'monster' and of the failure of the Invisibility Task Force to perform the necessary memory charms on all of them. The newsletter does mention that Hagrid has offered to keep the kelpie in the Hogwarts lake; the problem is that the Ministry hasn't been able to catch the beast.

I would have loved to have caught a glimpse of whatever it is. But even without a monster head sticking up out of the water, Loch Ness is a beautiful sight. I stopped along the rocky shore and skipped stones, looking across the water shimmering in the sunshine. I had always thought that it should be fairly easy for scientists to find a huge creature living in a lake, but I realised as I stood on the water's edge that this wasn't the case. Loch Ness is very large and, as I learned later at the visitors' centre, very deep and murky, containing more fresh water than all the lakes in England and Wales combined. That's a lot of space for the monster to hide in.

Sadly, this monster remained hidden as I drove the twenty miles to the end of the Loch. I finally came back to the castle just as the sun was going down. No monster. I guess the Ministry of Magic was on the job.

✦ Azkaban Fortress ✦

Azkaban was one place I wasn't sure I did want to find. Not the Azkaban in the books, anyway. Rowling has said in interviews that it is located on an island in the north of the North Sea, but that's not what makes it such a bad place. Until they revolted in book six, Dementors guarded the prison there, and I had no desire to meet any Dementors: these dreadful creatures drain all the happiness out of a person, and even Muggles, though they can't see them, can feel the effects of their presence.

I did want to find out what the 'north of the North Sea' was like, though, so I took a long bus ride up the coast from Inverness to a little town called John o' Groats. When I arrived, I had the same reaction that many travellers have when they reach this point: is this it? There isn't much there, to be honest, just a hotel and a few other buildings, along with a jetty where a ferry will take visitors across the sea to the Orkney Islands some seven or eight miles away. I wasn't sure if this was really the North Sea, since the boundary between that and the Atlantic is a bit ambiguous, but I figured it would be close enough for me to get some idea of the kind of island where Azkaban is found. I boarded the ferry and put on my life jacket. The sun was shining, the birds were soaring overhead, and I was looking forward to a nice, peaceful voyage.

The entire trip took the better part of an hour. Once we were away from the shore, the bright sunshine gave way quickly to rain squalls

FIGURE 104 *(left)*
A balmy morning off the northern coast of Scotland

FIGURE 105 *(right)*
The cliffs of Hoy, some of the tallest in Britain

and strong winds. I'm sure that the waves wouldn't have seemed particularly large to the crew of the boat, but as the wind picked up and the weather closed in, they seemed absolutely huge to me. They dwarfed the ferry as they rolled toward us, and when they struck they sprayed water all over the upper deck.

The bad weather blew itself out as quickly as it had come and by the time we were approaching the islands, the sun was shining again. The sparsely populated island of Hoy announced itself with a line of massive cliffs, some of the highest in Britain. Somewhere on Hoy, I knew, was a chamber carved out of a large chunk of rock which is the reputed home, depending on which legend you read, of either a dwarf called Trolld or a pair of giants who used their teeth to chew their way out when they were trapped in the stone. The island is also famous in Norse mythology as the site of an eternal battle, where warriors killed during the day are resurrected by magic overnight to fight again the next day, over and over again. It sounded like quite a place. I wouldn't have time to visit Hoy, however. My tour would take me between two other, more populated islands; I hoped they would be as interesting.

I needn't have worried. All of the Orkney Islands are utterly fascinating. Evidence of ancient inhabitants is everywhere, from standing stones every few hundred yards to the incredible remains of the five thousand-year-old village of Skara Brae. The wind never lets up and the weather changes from rain to sunshine then back to rain and fog within minutes. The landscape is low hills with barely any trees at all to break the wind. Orkney consists of about seventy

islands, some of which are 'skerries', barely more than scraps of rock poking above the waves. One of the smaller islands might be the magically-hidden Isle of Drear, which the books describe as the home of the extremely dangerous Quintapeds. I wouldn't be able to find it, however: according to *Fantastic Beasts and Where To Find Them*, wizards made Drear 'Unplottable' because they didn't want anyone accidentally going there and being slaughtered by the island's five-legged monsters.

Almost all of the human inhabitants of the Orkneys, however, live on a handful of the largest islands. I travelled around these islands by bus, stopping along the way for a nice lunch in the town of Stromness on the Mainland, as the largest Orkney island is known. I explored the towns and walked around ancient stone circles. As the bus wended its way around the larger islands, the wind blew constantly and the rain came and went.

MAGICAL PLACE

Azkaban Fortress

Location: On an island in the north of the North Sea.

Function: The wizarding prison where witches and wizards are held captive and guarded by Dementors, evil creatures who leach good feelings out of the prisoners.

How to get there: You don't want to get there, or if you do, you'll be more interested in how to get back. Cornelius Fudge mentioned that he flew there (and described the flight as miserable); this suggests that Azkaban isn't on the Floo Network of fireplaces. Sirius Black, in his Animagus dog form, managed to swim from the island to the mainland of Britain.

Description: The fortress itself is grim and forbidding, although we have no physical descriptions of it in the books.

Additional details: A plot of land outside the fortress walls has been set aside as a graveyard, where the Dementors bury the remains of prisoners who have died (GF27).

FIGURE 106 *Skara Brae's 5000-year-old ruins*

FIGURE 107 *One of the many ancient stone monuments in the Orkneys*

FIGURE 108 *A stop for lunch in Stromness, Orkney Islands*

Azkaban wouldn't be located on any of these large islands, I knew. No, it would be found in the middle of nowhere, probably not part of the Orkneys at all. Maybe it would be far out to the east of the Orkney Islands, a skerry all alone and buffeted by these extreme winds and pounded by waves. It would certainly be a terrible place to be imprisoned, isolated and completely surrounded by a cold, wild sea. On my return voyage, watching a sea bird hovering over the deck motionless in the stiff breeze, I wondered whether the birds even dared go near Azkaban. Probably not. Dementors would scare away anyone…and anything.

FIGURE 109 *Sea bird motionless over the ferry in the stiff breeze*

Hogwarts School of
Witchcraft and Wizardry

And now, finally, I was going to go look for Hogwarts Castle.

There are in fact quite a few castles tucked away next to tiny lochs or atop craggy hills in the Highlands. Most are crumbling ruins now. During my exploration of the Highlands, I encountered so many that I couldn't begin to visit them all. However, I was driving along the road near Loch Assynt when I saw ahead of me the stony ruins of what had once been a castle, and decided to take a look around. The ruins of this castle, called Ardvreck, stood by a small loch on a rocky jut of land which was almost an island; nearby I saw the ruins of what appeared to be a manor house.

The ground leading to the castle from the car park was springy and boggy, but once I walked out onto the peninsula I discovered solid ground criss-crossed with stone foundations and low walls. The castle must at one time have been a very impressive structure, though all that remains now are a few walls and a queerly-shaped tower protruding from a collapsed heap. Surprisingly, the dungeon is still visible at the base of the pile, which was very cool. Unfortunately the hole was closed off with steel bars, so I couldn't go poking around.

Ardvreck was built around 1590 by the MacLeod clan. According to history, in 1650 the Marquis of Montrose sought refuge there after losing a battle against the Scottish Government, only to be tricked into entering the dungeon and being imprisoned there by the Lady of the castle. She called in the troops and he was dragged off to Edinburgh to be hanged, drawn and quartered.

The legends about the castle are just as interesting as the history. The ghost of a tall man is said to wander the third floor, of which barely a few crumbling square feet now remain. Perhaps this is the ghost of Montrose himself, trying to escape the dungeon several now-vanished floors below. The ghost of a small girl is also said to wander the ruins; legend suggests that the original builder of Ardvreck, probably one of the MacLeods, made a pact with the Devil to ensure the successful construction of the castle. The deal involved the clansman giving his daughter to the Devil to take as a wife. Upon learning of this bargain, the poor girl threw herself from the tower rather than go through with it. Can't say I blame her.

The manor house several hundred yards away is a mere shell, a few peaked stone walls and empty windows. How it came to be built near the castle and how it came to be destroyed are each interesting tales. In 1726, Ardvreck Castle was inhabited by Kenneth Mackenzie. His wife didn't care much for the place, however, and so he built her Calda House nearby to live in. I can just imagine the arguments, and Kenneth finally throwing up his hands and saying: "Fine, I'll build you a house!" To be fair, I can see her point. Living in a draughty old stone castle could hardly be called comfortable. According to some versions of the tale, the two residences proved too much of a strain on his finances and Mackenzie was brought to ruin. The house itself mysteriously burned down in 1737, supposedly due to divine retribution when a Mackenzie family celebration lasted past midnight on a Saturday evening and into the early hours of the Sabbath. The entire family was killed.

I loved Ardvreck, with its crumbling walls and dungeons, but it was much too small to be Hogwarts, even if you add in the manor house. I visited other castles in Scotland, but still none fit the bill.

FIGURES 110 & 111
Ruins of Ardvreck (left) and Duntulm Castles

I scrambled over the ruins of Duntulm, a castle built on a rocky promontory on the Isle of Skye, erected on top of the remains of three previous strongholds dating back to the Stone Age. Not much is left of Duntulm except a few walls and rumours that it is haunted, as most castles seem to be; but even at its most impressive, Duntulm would barely encompass one of the Hogwarts classrooms. Several days after my visit to the Isle of Skye, I walked through the ornately decorated rooms and halls of Blair Castle, still occupied by the Duke of Atholl (when he's not living in South Africa, that is). His castle is protected by the Atholl Highlanders, the only legal private army in Europe. Blair Castle is more of a manor house than a castle, if truth be told, but even so it can't come close to matching the grandeur of Hogwarts.

Many more castles are to be found in the Highlands, each with their own legends and histories. Some are almost entirely in ruins, like Ardvreck and Duntulm; others are still intact and even inhabited like Blair. Rowling herself has said that Duart Castle on the Isle of Mull provided inspiration for Hogwarts, and it's easy to see why: Duart Castle is a grand sight, perched as it is on an outcrop of rock next to the water. However, even the grandest Scottish castle

FIGURE 112 *Blair Castle*

FIGURE 113 *Duart Castle on the Isle of Mull in Scotland*
(*image courtesy Undiscovered Scotland, www.undiscoveredscotland.co.uk*)

can't match the sheer size and towering height of the castle where Harry Potter lives and attends school.

A castle the size of Hogwarts, with the main buildings standing seven storeys high and towers soaring still higher, simply doesn't exist in the Highlands, and certainly wasn't possible in the 900s when according to the books Hogwarts was built. Stone castles weren't even built in Britain until after the Norman Conquest in the 11th century. Before that, the closest thing would be a hill fort with earthworks or a timbered hall. In fact, there wasn't even anything you could call a town in Scotland until the 12th century. But no matter. Hogwarts was constructed and concealed by wizards using magic, after all; architecturally, the Wizarding world could have been ahead of its time.

As I said, if I was going to hide a castle, large or small, I would definitely choose the Highlands as the place to do it, just as Rowling did when she invented her magical school for young witches and wizards. Now the trick was going to be to find the most likely location. Fortunately, the books do offer a few clues to where this might be.

The students attending the school leave King's Cross Station at eleven o'clock in the morning on the first of September, travel north aboard the Hogwarts Express steam train, and arrive after dark at a solitary railway station about half a mile from the castle. Hogwarts itself is located on the shores of a lake with a forest nearby and mountains visible all around. Given the lateness of sundown on the first of September and the speed of such a train, this journey would take them quite a way into Scotland, certainly well into the Highlands.

The Hogwarts Express is an interesting train indeed. One might wonder why students need to travel all the way to London, to King's Cross, when it might be a lot closer for them to travel directly to Scotland. Near the school is the all-Wizarding town of Hogsmeade. Certainly some of the students live there, or nearby. Wouldn't it be a lot more logical and convenient for them simply to walk to school?

That's Muggle logic, though. For wizards, a trip to Diagon Alley in London requires nothing more than stepping into a fireplace with a pinch of Floo Powder. The flames will flare up green and transport the wizard instantly into another fireplace in or near Diagon Alley. London is as close as the castle next door for a witch or wizard.

So why do they travel to London to catch the Hogwarts Express? Simply because that's where the train leaves from. Geographic distances aren't really a factor at all. In addition, Diagon Alley is where everyone goes to buy their supplies for the year, their books and robes and wands and who knows what. For a wizard, London is a perfectly reasonable place to start the journey.

There's also a social reason why all the students would travel together. The tradition of a school train hired to transport students was not invented by Rowling. During the twentieth century, many boarding schools in Britain used hired school trains to fetch all of the pupils at once to begin the school year. Pico Iyer, writing about the first Harry Potter book in the New York Times, compared the trip to Diagon Alley to buy supplies and the journey on the Hogwarts Express to his own experiences going to boarding school in Britain:

> Here are all the rites I remember as vividly as lemon drops: the cryptic list of instructions that would appear through the mail, describing what we must – and mustn't – bring to school (the point of all the rules being not to make order so much as to enforce obedience);

the trip to dusty old shops with creaky family names – New & Lingwood or Alden & Blackwell – where aged men would fit us out with the approved uniform and equipment, as they had done for our fathers and our fathers' fathers; the special school train that would be waiting in a London station to transport us to our cells. Once the doors clanged shut behind us, we knew we were inside an alternative reality where none of the usual rules applied – and where there was only one sex, everyone wore tails every day and it was assumed that every boy would partake of Anglican worship twice a day.

In Rowling's world, the children gather in one place for their farewells, board the school train, and find themselves transported together to a magical alternate reality. On the journey, they discuss the summer holidays and the school year to come. They wrangle their places in the social milieu of Hogwarts, sorting out who are their friends and who are the 'wrong sort'. By the time they disembark on the tiny Highland railway platform, they are acclimatised, as it were, and ready to begin their new school year in their school home.

It's certainly possible to take a similar journey to Scotland. Every day at noon, a train leaves from King's Cross heading for the Scottish Highlands. There's also an overnight train, the Caledonian Sleeper, which departs Euston Station at 9:15 in the evening and arrives the next morning; while this doesn't match the journey of the Hogwarts Express, it does have the added romance of sleeping on a moving train. But, of course, neither train calls at Hogsmeade, and Hogsmeade Station and Hogwarts castle are hardly going to appear on any maps.

The station's position, however, did give me something to go on. In the books, the Hogwarts Express terminates in the Scottish Highlands at Hogsmeade Station, a lonely platform about half a mile from the lake and forest. I think it's fair to assume that this station would be very remote, far from Muggle eyes. So I pored over the map, following the railway line on as it crosses the Highlands, looking for a likely location. Of course, being a magical train, the Hogwarts Express may not travel on the normal Muggle rail lines and so the station might not correspond to a real station at all, but for the sake of this exploration I decided to assume it does.

As I traced the railway line on the map, however, I realised that most of the stations in the Highlands simply won't work. They're typically located near villages or very close to Muggle roads and buildings. After all, why build a station if there aren't any people around to use it? It was going to be be tricky to find a remote station that isn't in the middle of Muggle territory. Following the rails on a map revealed another problem: with very few exceptions, the line follows roads along its entire route through Scotland. It seems unlikely that Hogsmeade and Hogwarts are to be found near a Muggle highway any more than they would be very near a Muggle town.

Then I spotted something unexpected, something interesting. At Loch Tulla, the West Highland Railway veers from the A82 and travels across the moors until it joins the A86 heading to Fort William. So for about thirty miles the line meanders across Rannoch Moor far from roads and villages. To my delight, I saw that along this desolate stretch of track are two lonely stations.

I did a little research and discovered that one of these, Corrour Station, is known as the most remote station in Scotland. Originally built to service the Corrour hunting and shooting estate, it has no public roads leading to it whatsoever. It's located near Loch Ossian, a beautiful narrow loch with a forest spreading right down to the water. The other station along this route is Rannoch Station, which is quite near Loch Laidon. A road, albeit a small one, travels the forty-odd miles to Rannoch Station from the A9, but the road ends at the station. I looked back at the map, feeling a little thrill. Either of these could be a good candidate for Hogsmeade Station. I might just be getting close to Hogwarts.

But would this location work with the schedule of the Hogwarts Express in the books? I checked the timetables online. The 'real' train from King's Cross, which leaves at noon and requires one change of trains, arrives at Rannoch just after nine in the evening and at Corrour some fifteen minutes later. Assuming that the Hogwarts Express follows the same route, without a change of trains, but that it travels somewhat slower than a modern train, the magical steam train would also arrive around nine p.m. This works out just fine, since the books tell us that the students disembark in the dark; sunset on the first of September in that part of the world is a little past eight o'clock at night.

HOGSMEADE STATION

According to the books, when the students arrive in Scotland aboard the Hogwarts Express, they disembark at a small railway station. The platform is described as 'tiny'. Considering the length of the Hogwarts Express, which accommodates well over three hundred passengers, the platform must actually be fairly long. Perhaps it just seemed tiny to Harry, crammed as it was with all those kids. From the platform, the first-year students follow Hagrid down a steep narrow path in the dark until they come to the edge of a lake. Older students follow the platform to a muddy path where stagecoaches pulled by invisible horses wait to take them around the lake to the castle.

My journey to Scotland wasn't aboard a magical steam train; once again, I had to rely on a very un-magical rented car. I checked the map and saw that the single road to Rannoch Station left the A9 near Pitlochry and headed off along the north side of Loch Trummel and Loch Rannoch. I set off, expecting it would take me about an hour to drive the forty-odd miles from the A9 to the station.

I hadn't anticipated the type of road. I shouldn't have been surprised: I was looking for somewhere remote, after all, and I didn't expect a superhighway. However, this road was barely one lane wide and wound its way through forests and along mountainsides. Each curve was an adventure. I had no idea what sort of vehicle I might meet coming the other way and when I did, both of us had to squeeze against the bushes at the edge of the road to pass.

I wasn't half way through the journey when I started to wonder if I was making a huge mistake. After all, I had no idea if this station would actually fit the description in the books. The maps showed that it was near a loch, but that didn't mean much – just about everywhere in the Highlands is fairly near some loch or other. What I had thought of as a quick jaunt was turning out to be quite an excursion into the wilderness. I was glad I had a full tank of petrol.

The road became even narrower as I drove along. Thankfully, the number of other vehicles on the road dropped to almost zero. This was a good thing, not only because it made me feel safer driving but

FIGURE 114 *The road became narrower the farther I travelled*

NOT-SO-MAGICAL PLACE

Hogsmeade Station

Location: Along the railway line near a lake.

Function: The destination of the Hogwarts Express, where students disembark to travel on to the school.

How to get there: The train, obviously, but also a road which winds around the lake, through the gates into the Hogwarts grounds, and beyond that to Hogsmeade village.

Description: The platform is 'tiny', which leaves us with the mystery of how they disembark three hundred passengers onto it in a short time, along with trunks and owls.

Additional details: The station is not anywhere near the village of Hogsmeade, which we see in the map Rowling drew of the area and showed to the camera in an interview on the DVD of *Harry Potter and the Prisoner of Azkaban*. This gives us some evidence that the station is on the Muggle railway line. The village of Hogsmeade, a completely magical town, wouldn't be located near the Muggle station.

also because it signified that the station I was driving towards wasn't overly busy with Muggle traffic. I drove along the beautiful Loch Rannoch and then out across Rannoch Moor.

The railway line crosses Rannoch Moor as well, and that stretch of the West Highland line is considered one of the most beautiful in Scotland. Mountains surround the moor, which is boggy and wet with innumerable streams, lochs and lochlans (small lakes and ponds). The workers laying the track in the late 1800s faced a tremendous challenge as they tried to run the line across this forbidding, treacherous moor, as in many places there was simply no solid ground on which to lay the track bed. Eventually they came up with a very ingenious solution: they literally floated the track over the wet moorland on mats of brush-wood, tree roots and dirt. This doesn't seem to me like a particularly safe way to build a railway line, but since the tracks are still there and remain in use over a hundred

---

Source of information about Harry's world: The Daily Prophet newsletters

Written by: J.K. Rowling for a short-lived fan club in Britain.

Dates: The newsletters were written in 1998 and 1999, but the events described take place during the timeframe of the first three books, which is 1991–1993.

Description: The four issues of the Daily Prophet newsletters are each four pages long. They're written in Rowling's usual playful style and include several storylines which run from issue to issue. For example, a Chaser for the Montrose Magpies by the name of Alisdair Maddock becomes more and more fascinated with Muggle sports in issues one and two, leading to his sacking from the team in the third issue after having been 'caught' with a set of golf clubs. Some familiar Potter names appear for the first time in the newsletters, including Gwenog Jones and Dragon Pox.

Additional details: The newsletters were clearly written by Rowling before she had worked out every detail of her invented world, as some information is contradicted by later books. In a fun tie-in with the characters in the story, the 'For Sale' section of the second issue includes an advertisement by someone named A. Weasley who is selling a collection of batteries.

years later, their method evidently worked. However, the speed limit for trains crossing Rannoch Moor is thirty miles an hour to prevent damage to the track.

As I drove across it, I could see that Rannoch Moor is quite different from Dartmoor. In Devon, the moorland had been raised above the surrounding countryside, bleak and barren. Here in Scotland, the moor is surrounded by mountains, almost like the bottom of a very large bowl. This area is said to be one of the last true wild places in Scotland.

In fact, it's so wild and forbidding that it is famous in history and legend as a place where people could hide away from whomever might be looking for them. During the 1600s, Rannoch was home to bands of brigands and marauders, including a rogue element of the MacGregor clan, who would attack peaceful homesteads of rival clans and then escape into the wilderness. This problem lingered for years despite the best efforts of the authorities because Rannoch proved to be such a perfect place to hide away.

One such hiding place was a man-made island in Loch Rannoch itself. This island, called a 'crannog', was constructed by floating mats of reeds out into the loch, then sinking them with stones. This was repeated over and over until an island was created, into which pilings were driven to hold a wooden fortified house. The crannog in Loch Rannoch was built with a sunken causeway leading out to it. Apart from the small boats of the time, the only way to reach the safety of the island was to know the path of the underwater walkway. Interestingly, the causeway doesn't lead from the nearer shore as one might expect. This is because the water between the crannog and the closest shoreline is unexpectedly deep.

Rannoch Moor is also famous in cartoons and comic books as the location of the castle home of Scrooge McDuck, the wealthy uncle of Donald Duck. No doubt the folks who wrote those stories chose Rannoch Moor because of its reputation for being remote, inhospitable and very mysterious. As I drove along the narrow road, I thought that this reputation was well deserved.

I drove past Rannoch Moor and crossed a few bridges. The morning was nearly gone when I found myself in a wooded stretch of road, barely a mile or two from my destination. There ahead of me I saw a sign that warned 'No road beyond Rannoch Station'. Well, this was a good sign – of course there's no road if instead there's a magical castle just beyond, on the lake. However, if the place was going to be similar to Hogsmeade Station and Hogwarts, there would have to be some kind of road, a track at least, which the carriages would follow to take the students to their school. I would soon know. I drove the remaining distance with mounting excitement.

The car park near the station was all but deserted. Ahead of me I could see a pedestrian overpass, typical of railway stations, allowing people access to either side of the tracks. I couldn't see the station itself until I started climbing the stairs of the overpass and looked to my right. What I saw took my breath away.

Rannoch Station *was* Hogsmeade Station. It was small and quaint, exactly the way I had pictured the station in the books. The green roofs were topped with several chimneys. The platform was fairly short with tracks on either side. In the distance all around were mountains and hills. As I stood on the overpass following the tracks with my eyes to where they joined on the far side of the station, I could see a viaduct just beyond, heading north. I'd read about that viaduct, which had been built to take the tracks over an area of bog which simply wouldn't support them any other way.

I savoured the view. Then I noticed that a plaque had been placed on the overpass. I read it carefully.

'At 1000 feet above sea level,' it read, 'the 56 square miles of Rannoch Moor provide one of the wildest and most forbidding landscapes in Scotland. Treacherous mires, boulder strewn moorland, complete lack of shelter and an exposure to wind and rain, make this an inhospitable environment. It is a constantly changing landscape transforming itself according to the light, the weather and the season.'

That certainly sounded like the kind of place to hide Hogwarts castle. I read on.

'Walkers are warned that this is not an area to trifle with. The distances between shelter, habitation and stations are great and there have been regular instances of people getting lost or stuck in peat bogs. Rannoch abounds with legends, folk tales and stories of witches, ghosts, and the supernatural.'

FIGURE 115
The approach to Rannoch Station

FIGURE 116
Rannoch Station

FIGURE 117 *Looking towards the loch from Rannoch Station*

MAGICAL CREATURES OF SCOTLAND

A number of magical creatures are known to live in the wilds of Scotland. Many of them are found in the forests and lochs near Hogwarts itself and are cared for there by Hagrid, the Hogwarts gamekeeper.

Acromantulas These massive and very dangerous spiders are actually native to Borneo. However, over fifty years ago Hagrid raised one named Aragog in the castle and released it into the Forbidden Forest. He found a mate for Aragog named Mosag, and the two Acromantulas founded a colony in the forest. They are probably the most deadly creatures to be found in the forest around Hogwarts. The Death Eaters recruited them to fight against the castle in the Battle of Hogwarts.

Centaurs Wise and intelligent, these secretive creatures have the body of a horse and the torso and head of a human. The herd of Centaurs living in the Hogwarts forest is led by Magorian and Ronan. The Centaurs tried to remain neutral during the war but eventually joined in the battle against Voldemort.

Hippogriffs The forest around Hogwarts is also the home of a number of Hippogriffs. These strange creatures were probably bred by magic, as they have the head of an eagle and the body of a horse. Hagrid kept one, Buckbeak, as a pet.

Unicorns Another horse-like creature living in the forest is the unicorn. These beautiful and shy animals are pure white in colour and have a single horn on their forehead.

The map in the centre of the plaque showed the entire area, and sure enough, there was a loch quite nearby, although it was hidden by trees from where I was standing. I also noticed drawings of what looked like giants holding large boulders over their heads. I would have to find out what that was all about. I walked back down onto the platform of the station and looked off in the direction that the map showed the loch.

I do realise that Rowling probably never looked at a map of Scotland when she invented her magical school. I'm pretty sure that she didn't triangulate exactly where a solitary station stood suitably far from a lot of Muggle activity in the midst of the Highlands, near all the right geographical features. I'm certain she never took the train and watched the scenery, hoping to spot a place that fitted perfectly. But if she *had* done all that, I'm convinced that she could very well have ended up here. She would have taken one look at Rannoch

Thestrals Over a hundred of these grotesque but useful flying horses live in the Hogwarts forest. On the first day of term, the thestrals pull the carriages from Hogsmeade Station up the road to the castle. Only someone who has seen death can see a thestral, so many of the students assume that the carriages pull themselves. Thestrals are 'skeletal' and black, with bat-like wings.

Giant Squid How a giant squid managed to find itself living in a freshwater lake in the middle of the Scottish Highlands is anyone's guess, but the specimen living in the lake near Hogwarts is surprisingly intelligent and gentle. Students have been known to pet its tentacles and feed it toast.

Merpeople The lake is also the home of a colony of Merfolk, led by Merchieftainess Murcus. Their village is located in the deepest part of the lake. Scottish merpeople are called Selkies.

Grindylows Grindylows are pale green creatures with long spindly fingers. Always a danger to swimmers in the lake, grindylows are fond of grabbing at ankles and pulling people to their death.

Kelpies – Many varieties of these gregarious, shape-changing creatures exist in lakes, rivers, and wells. The largest in Scotland lives in Loch Ness and is a huge problem for the wizarding community as it is very fond of showing off and scaring Muggles.

SOURCE: The novels and *Fantastic Beasts and Where to Find Them*

Station and beyond that, at the view to the lake and mountains and trees and thought, this is it. It has to be.

I was looking at Hogwarts. Not the castle, of course, since that would be invisible to me even if it were real, but the lake and mountains and forests where the castle would be. What I was seeing as I gazed across the rolling hills toward the distant mountains was absolutely perfect. About half a mile away was a loch, shimmering in the sun, which stretched off into the distance to the left. On the far side of this loch, the slopes of a mountain came down almost to the shore. A forest of pines covered the hillside, dark and silent. I couldn't tell if there was a path because the ground between the station and the lake was quite hilly.

It's not very much like the view in the films, though. For the films, the producers chose a truly spectacular setting at the end of Loch Shiel quite a few miles further along the railway line. I had visited there myself and the view is beyond belief. The loch stretches off into the distance between steep mountainsides. Small islands dot the end of the loch, almost too picturesque to be real. The special effects department took this view and perched the castle on a beautiful peninsula that juts out into the water.

FIGURE 118 *Loch Shiel*

When I had visited Loch Shiel, I had stood on top of a steep hillside and looked at that scene. I could imagine Harry flying down that stretch of water on Buckbeak the Hippogriff, between the green mountains reaching down into the lake, the way he does in the third film. What doesn't show in the film, however, is that at the water's edge stands a tall monument to Bonnie Prince Charlie. A major highway passes within a few hundred yards of the monument, and the car park and gift shop nearby are usually filled with tourists. The special effects department must have used movie magic to erase all that from the film.

The monument is only one of the enticements for tourists, however. I had followed the signs through the thick wet grass and climbed a hillside to see the view, and when I turned around, away from Loch Sheil and the monument, I saw another incredible sight, also straight from the Harry Potter films: the great curved Glenfinnen Viaduct. That's the same curving railway bridge that shows up in several of the films, including the memorable scene in the second movie where Harry and Ron drive the flying Ford Anglia right into the path of the train as it thunders up behind them.

FIGURE 119 *Glenfinnen Viaduct*

Hogwarts School of Witchcraft and Wizardry

Location: The Highlands of Scotland, near Hogsmeade Station and the village of Hogsmeade.

Function: A school for magical young people to learn the skills they need to become 'fully qualified' witches and wizards.

How to get there: Typically, students arrive by means of the Hogwarts Express school train, but the Knight Bus does stop at the gates on occasion. It is not possible to Apparate directly into the school grounds, but it is possible to Apparate into the nearby village. The school fireplaces are sometimes connected to the Floo Network. At one time there were seven secret passages out of the castle, but many of them are now blocked.

Description (outside): The castle is huge, with seven storeys and a number of towers rising above that. A dark forest and a large lake dominate the grounds. There are mountains all around. A Quidditch pitch is located near the castle.

Description (inside): A 'vast' entrance hall is dominated by a marble staircase which leads to the upper floors. To the right as one enters by the oak front doors is the Great Hall, with four long house tables and a raised dais at the front where the teachers sit. Classrooms, dormitories, and other rooms fill the castle. There is a hospital wing and a library.

Additional details: Around 990 AD, the 'four greatest witches and wizards of the age' built Hogwarts to train students far from harassment by Muggles. The castle has other inhabitants besides the students, including more than twenty ghosts, a poltergeist named Peeves, and a crotchety old caretaker named Filch. Rowling has mentioned that she was inspired for the look of the castle by Duart Castle on the Isle of Mull.

Of course, these are stunning views and they look fantastic in the films. However, the real Hogwarts simply couldn't be located here. The whole place is crawling with Muggles, viewing the monument, climbing the hill to get a good look at the viaduct, or just driving past in their cars admiring the view. There is no railway station nearby either; Glenfinnen Station is a mile or two farther up the road. No matter how beautiful Loch Shiel is, it can't be the location of Hogwarts.

I stood on that pedestrian bridge looking out at Rannoch Station and compared what I saw to Loch Shiel. The loch near Rannoch Station, Loch Laidon, was isolated and pretty much Muggle-free. The Muggle road ends at the station. The loch is located in the middle of nowhere on a moor that's known as one of the most inhospitable wild places in Scotland, a place which was described as rife with 'legends, folk tales and stories of witches, ghosts, and the supernatural.' The plaque even promised that there were giants in this area. Even though it wasn't quite as picturesque, Loch Laidon was a much more likely place for Hogwarts.

I descended the steps and walked up and down the station platform, imagining the bright red steam engine pulling up from the south and the crowd of excited students disembarking to begin the last leg of their journey. From the train, the students would walk to the waiting carriages. That would take them back into the car park, I calculated. Where would they go from there? I looked beyond the trees and saw that, sure enough, a small gravel lane led from the car park, across the tracks just down from the station, and through a gate onto the moor, leading in the direction of the lake. I walked back over the pedestrian bridge and traced the route with my eyes. I wondered if it was forbidden for people to take that path. The gate was closed, from what I could see.

I would have to ask someone. I went back onto the platform and into the small station, where I discovered a very pleasant tea room. I ordered a cup of coffee and noticed the books for sale: *Tales of Rannoch* and *A History of Rannoch*, both by a local writer named Alec Cunningham. I bought them both, then took my coffee out onto the platform where there were a few picnic tables. I opened *Tales of Rannoch*: sure enough, the book explained the giants depicted on the station plaque. The story told of two ill-tempered giants living just on the other side of that mountain ahead of me, who took turns showing off how far they could throw rocks. A clever local fellow had goaded them into this contest, which continued until the two giants were so exhausted that they collapsed and died, much to the relief of the local people. The story was used to explain the large number of boulders and rocks scattered over the terrain here. Nowadays the geologists tell us that those boulders were left behind by glaciers, but I prefer the giant story.

I finished my coffee, then went back in to ask the fellow running the tea shop if it was allowed to walk towards the loch. Of course, he told me. Just follow the path. I thanked him, trying not to sound too excited, stepped back out onto the platform, and set off towards... Hogwarts.

FIGURE 120 *The road towards the moor*

FIGURE 121 *The gravel lane leading away from the station*

HOGWARTS CASTLE

I crossed back over the pedestrian bridge and into the car park. The gravel road led towards the moor, blocked by a metal gate. A couple of hikers were walking toward me and I was tempted to ask if they'd seen anything mysterious or magical, but decided against it.

I pushed through the gate and onto the road beyond. As I started down the path, I thought about the stories in the books and tried to think about how they fitted with what I was seeing. I was a bit concerned that the lake and the road would be very visible to any Muggles who happened to be hanging around the station. It seemed to me that Hogwarts should be somewhat hidden, out of view, and this lane looked very exposed. I was wrong, though. The gravel path wound between small hills and sloped downward so that by the time I was a hundred yards past the tracks, I could barely see the station at all, or the lake either for that matter. The undulating landscape and tall grasses blocked the view almost as effectively as the hedgerows of Devon.

FIGURE 122 *The station is barely visible from the path*

The path curved around the end of the lake and soon I found myself close to the forest which covered the mountainside to my right. The forest near Hogwarts is sometimes called The Forbidden Forest and is filled with all sorts of strange and dangerous creatures.

FIGURE 123 *The forest and a fence along the loch*

On the few occasions that Harry has entered it, he has found it very difficult to walk through because of the thick trees and bushes and the uneven, root-covered ground. The forest I was looking at certainly measured up. I tried to see into it, but the pine trees were too thick and the shadows between them too dark. Even if I had been able to scramble up the embankment at the edge of the path, I doubted than I would have been able to get very far into those trees. I remembered the Acromantulas and Centaurs and Grawp the Giant, all of whom the books said lived in the Forbidden Forest. As I looked into the dark trees, I could easily imagine dangerous creatures looking back at me from the shadows. I also thought about the more down to earth dangers mentioned on that plaque back at the station, and decided to stay on the path.

The lane curved still further until I was on the other side of the lake. A fence ran along the path here, separating me from the water by a good hundred yards. I had hoped to walk down to the shore and look around, but there was no way to do that.

According to the books, if Muggles get too near to Hogwarts, they'll see a mouldering ruin with a sign warning them to keep out, that the building is unsafe. I wondered if there might be a ruin along the shore on the other side of that fence, perhaps hidden among the low hills.

The books also say that because of the enchantments on the place, Muggles who get too close will suddenly remember something that they had to do and leave. Not me, though. There was no other place I wanted to be just now: I was going to find Hogwarts, and no Muggle-Repelling Charm was going to stop me.

I hadn't counted on a stout wire fence, though.

I stopped and looked around, and thought through the description again. The book describes Hogwarts as standing on top of a high mountain next to the lake. There was a high mountain here, rising up to my right, covered with forest, but it was too high and set too far back from the water to fit the book description. I'd have to settle for imagining the low hills beside me as the location of the castle. Indeed, the fence seemed to be surrounding a fairly tall hill just ahead of me, on the shore of the loch. The gravel road wound between that hill and the forest. I kept walking.

I wasn't sure what I was actually looking for. Just like my search for Grimmauld Place and St Mungo's, I wanted to be surprised. I wanted to find something unexpected, I guess, something that would tell me that I'd arrived. A building, maybe. A ruined building. Pillars with winged boars on the top would do. Better yet, a giant gamekeeper named Hagrid, tramping along toward the forest to check on the local wildlife. All I knew was that I wanted to find something, something that would tell me that I had found what I was looking for.

The lane stretched out ahead of me, between Loch Laidon and the mountain, and I suddenly found myself at a fork in the road. Off to the left, towards the lake, a two-track road ran off on the other side of the fence, around the hill. The road was blocked by a wooden gate, securely fastened. On the fence post was a simple sign, hand-painted, that said 'PRIVATE'. I stopped.

Had that sign been painted by Hagrid? If I pushed that gate open and followed the road around that hill, would I find myself looking at a mouldering ruin with a sign saying 'Dangerous Building – Keep Out'? Would I discover a Quidditch pitch and a dangerous old Whomping Willow tree? Or would I suddenly remember an appointment I had somewhere and wander off, the victim of a Muggle-Repelling Charm?

FIGURE 124 *The end of the road*

I stood there in the middle of that gravel path, staring at the sign and the closed gate. Behind me I could hear the breeze in the branches of the trees of the forest. The sun shone on the water beyond the fence and the hill, and I thought about the station and the moor and my long trip across the Highlands to find this place. What was I looking for? I put my hand on the gate and considered that question. Was I really looking for a castle that doesn't exist? Partly, I realised. I wanted to see Hogwarts, actually see it, rising majestically on top of that hill or just around that bend.

Honestly, though, that wasn't what I wanted. I know that Hogwarts only exists in the pages of the Harry Potter books, and that's fine, that's enough. So what was I looking for? What would bring an otherwise sane person far into the wilderness to stand next to a small loch and stare at a fence and a gate and a sign?

I wanted to find magic. Real magic. The kind of magic that comes from reading an extraordinary story filled with imaginative creatures, characters and places. The kind of magic that comes from experiencing first-hand a little bit of that fantastic world in the real-life places the author describes. The kind of magic that comes to life in Devon and London and New Mills and in the Highlands of Scotland because it's the magic of imagination.

I knew I was there, where I wanted to be, and that I'd found what I was looking for. I had found the magic of a truly beautiful, enchanting part of the world, and, at the same time, found the mystery of the invented world of Harry Potter that always stayed just out of reach, just a little way beyond where cars and trains and my feet could take me. I looked at that sign and I knew that I didn't need to go any farther. Whatever was beyond that last curve of the road was indeed private. I didn't need to go there to know what it was. I'd found my magic.

FIGURE 125 *The magic of the Scottish Highlands*

NOW WHERE?

Is that the end of the road? Are my travels over? I hope not. After all, there are still Harry Potter places to discover. I hadn't found the rock out in the sea where Harry and the Dursleys first meet Hagrid, for example. I wanted to fly to Albania and see what the forests look like, although finding just the right hollow tree where Voldemort hid the Diadem of Ravenclaw might be asking a bit much.

That's not all, though. Even with the places I had visited, there is always more to explore and learn. Are there other places in Surrey that fit the bill for Little Whinging? New Mills was a great town to explore and there were elements that tallied with the description of Spinner's End, but surely there are other towns which might match. And I haven't yet found a place that works for Little Hangleton.

I'll keep looking and exploring. I have learned so much on my excursions around Britain. I've visited ancient villages and met interesting people. I've been told tales of ghosts and pixies, giants and witches. I've wandered the streets of London, the moors of Devon and the highlands of Scotland. Along the way, friends and acquaintances have offered advice and ideas, sometimes coming up with amazing insights and tidbits of information which have led me in new directions and brightened up my travels and this book.

So no, this isn't the end of the road. I know there will always be a little more magic to be found.

FIGURE 126 *...always a little more magic to be found...*

APPENDIX ONE

Getting Around
in the Wizarding World

✦

If you're a witch or wizard, you have a decided advantage when it comes to travel. It's true that some of the methods aren't quite as comfortable as their Muggle counterparts, but most of them are able to get you from point A to point B much more quickly. The Department of Magical Transportation, part of the Ministry of Magic, monitors and controls most of these methods. A few do slip by, though – a certain flying Ford Anglia comes to mind…

MAGIC SPELLS AND OBJECTS

✦ Apparition

Apparating, magically disappearing from one place and appearing almost instantaneously somewhere else, is a tricky bit of magic which is only allowed to be performed by those who can pass a test, administered by the Ministry. There's an Apparition Test Centre on the sixth floor of the Ministry of Magic and a twelve-week course is offered to sixth-year Hogwarts students by a Ministry Apparition Instructor. Harry describes the feeling of Apparating as being 'squeezed through a rubber tube'. Apparition gets more difficult the farther one Apparates, and no one attempts to do it from one continent to another – not even Voldemort, who flew back from his confrontation with Grindelwald at Nurmengard when he got the message that Harry had been captured. If the magic isn't performed correctly, a person might 'splinch' themselves, which means leaving part of themselves behind when they Apparate. This isn't typically fatal, surprisingly enough, but it requires quick work from the Accidental Magic Reversal Squad to fix things.

◆ Floo Powder

This magical powder is thrown into a fireplace which has been connected to the Floo Network of wizarding fireplaces. The flames burst up 'emerald green' and a person steps into them, saying the name of their destination. They spin and whirl and find themselves deposited out of the fireplace of the place they wanted to go.

◆ Portkey

A Portkey is an enchanted object, often a piece of apparently worthless junk, which when touched will transport a person to a pre-programmed location and at a pre-programmed time. An object can be transformed into a Portkey by the *Portus* spell.

◆ Broomsticks

A flying broomstick is not simply a "normal" broomstick pressed into service as a mode of transportation, but a magical item with built-in charms. The earliest known evidence of a broomstick enchanted to fly dates to 962 A.D.; brooms are thought to have been chosen because they are easily transported and concealed from Muggles. As time passed, they would also prove to be conducive to playing a number of sports. Flying on a broomstick, particularly one which accelerates as quickly as the Firebolt, must necessarily involve some form of magic protective field holding rider to broom and shielding against wind and inertial forces. Without this, it seems unlikely that anyone could hang on when a Firebolt accelerates from zero to 150 mph in only ten seconds. In years past, broomstick riders had to sit right on the handle, which was uncomfortable indeed. To alleviate this problem, Elliot Smethwyk invented the Cushioning Charm in 1820.

MAGICAL VEHICLES

◆ The Knight Bus

The Knight Bus is a magical 'triple-decker, violently purple bus' which will turn up to 'rescue' a witch or wizard who finds themselves stranded and in need of transportation. A seat on the Knight Bus can also be booked in advance for trips around Britain. The conductor of the Knight Bus is Stan Shunpike. The driver is Ernie Prang, an elderly wizard who doesn't seem to be able to see very well. In the film version, he is aided by a talking shrunken head hanging in the windscreen; this does not occur in the book, however.

The driver and conductor sit in the front of the bus in armchairs. During the night, there are no other seats on board; rather the Knight Bus provides a half a dozen brass bedsteads per level, which in the daytime are replaced by armchairs for the passengers. Lighting comes from candles in brackets on the walls. A small wooden staircase leads to the upper floors. The ride is very bumpy as the bus seems to jump erratically from one place to another. If you're not careful, you will find yourself thrown around the interior of the bus during its travels.

The fare from Little Whinging to London is eleven sickles. For an extra two sickles you get hot chocolate and if you pay two more besides, you get a hot water bottle and a toothbrush.

◆ Hogwarts Express

The Hogwarts Express is a passenger train which runs between King's Cross Station, London, and Hogsmeade Station at least four times a year, and probably more often than that, as needed. It does leave without fail on September 1 at eleven o'clock from Platform Nine and Three-Quarters, King's Cross, arriving at Hogsmeade Station in the early evening. Most students take the train back to King's Cross to go home for the Christmas and Easter holidays. The train also makes the run back again to London at the end of term in June.

The train is pulled by a scarlet steam locomotive. There is no dining service, but a witch pushes a tea trolley through the train midway through the journey, selling various types of sweets, snacks and iced pumpkin juice. There is a separate compartment or two at the front of the train for Hogwarts Prefects. There are usually no adults aboard the Hogwarts Express except the witch with the tea trolley and the driver.

Though it does look like one and acts like one in certain key ways, the Hogwarts Express, in all probability, is not really a steam train but a magical device. Like the Ministry cars, the Knight Bus, and Wizard's Wireless, it borrows its form and its intended function from real Muggle inventions, but not the technology. Wizarding "machines" aren't Muggle machines. They don't run on petrol or coal or electricity, they work by magic. In some cases, such as the Hogwarts Express, they are copied from Muggle machinery (and in this case it's clearly a copy of a Muggle device, since many parts of it would have no function in the wizarding version, but there they are, clearly copied from the Muggle original without an understanding of what those parts were for). The Hogwarts Express, powered by magic, chugs away up north because that's what it's supposed to do. Magic is, more than anything else, intention made reality.

So what about the track? Following the same pattern as the other magical transportation devices we've seen, the Knight Bus and the Ministry cars, I like the idea that the Hogwarts Express uses existing track for most of the journey, but just squeezes past the other trains on the line or cars at the crossings. It's not heard or seen by Muggles because, as Stan Shunpike points out about the Knight Bus, they simply don't notice magical things.

The driver and the guard and the witch with the cart are the equivalent of Ernie Prang and Stan Shunpike: trained to operate magical devices using magic without really understanding the technology from which their devices are copied. Ernie shifts the wheel back and forth but doesn't really steer the bus along the road specifically; he's making the magic work. One turn could send them to the left side of the motorway or halfway to Torquay, depending on what he intended it to do.

The train itself looks like a train from the outside and pretty much looks like a train on the inside, although I think it's likely that it adjusts its interior dimensions for the task at hand (there is always one more compartment for the students boarding the train, but never surplus, it seems). Unlike the Knight Bus, which looks fairly similar to a bus on the outside but nothing like a bus on the inside, the Hogwarts Express seems to be to most appearances a real train. But it isn't. It's magic.

✦ Ministry Cars

When it's necessary to travel around London in more traditional Muggle fashion, the Ministry of Magic can provide magical cars. These cars are much larger on the inside than on the outside and have a knack for moving through traffic very quickly.

✦ Boats to Hogwarts

When the first-year students arrive at Hogsmeade Station, they travel across the lake to the Hogwarts castle in a flotilla of small boats, propelled by magic.

✦ Flying carriage

A huge blue flying carriage was used by the Beauxbatons students to attend the Triwizard Tournament at Hogwarts. The carriage was drawn by twelve gigantic flying horses.

✦ Horseless carriages

About a hundred carriages wait along a rough mud road near Hogsmeade railway station on the first of September each year to take arriving Hogwarts students to school, returning them to the station at the beginning of the summer holidays. They are pulled by what Harry as a third- and fourth-year student assumed were invisible horses; this was verified at the beginning of his fifth year, when he first became aware of his ability to see thestrals. The thestrals who pull the carriages are very well-trained, since they make the journey unassisted past the wrought iron gates and around the Lake to the castle. The coaches smell of mould and straw.

✦ Gringotts cart

To reach the deep underground vaults of Gringotts Wizarding Bank in Diagon Alley, a goblin whistles for a small cart in which they and the visitor ride. The cart is self-propelled and apparently steers itself through the underground passages along railway tracks in the floor. The cart has only one speed: 'breakneck'.

✦ Magical ship

The students from Durmstrang arrived at Hogwarts for the Triwizard Tournament aboard a magical ship which surfaced in the centre of the Lake. It looks like a wreck that has been pulled up from the bottom of the sea, and appears to travel underwater.

MAGICAL FLYING ANIMALS

✦ Thestrals

Thestrals are huge, winged, skeletal horses with reptilian faces and necks. They are attracted to the smell of blood. Thestrals are invisible to anyone who has not seen death, which means that few of the students in Hagrid's Care of Magical Creatures classes could see them during Harry's fifth year. They are amazingly magical animals, however. People used to think they were bad omens, that seeing them meant bad luck, but this is just superstition. Thestrals have a magically accurate sense of direction and move magically fast through the air. Dumbledore used them to travel if he didn't care to Apparate (which probably explains how he got to the Ministry and maybe even how Hagrid got to the Hut on the Rock by flying). Harry and a group of students flew Thestrals from Hogwarts to the Ministry of Magic in an attempt to rescue Sirius .

The herd at Hogwarts started with a male and five females. A number of them have been born since, beginning with one named Tenebrus, which is a special favourite of Hagrid's. They are used to pull the school carriages from the train station up to the school.

✦ Hippogriffs

A flying creature with the head, wings, and forelegs of a giant eagle and the body (including hind legs and tail) of a horse, a Hippogriff can be used to transport a witch or wizard from place to place. The eyes are orange, while individual hippogriff colours vary much as those of mundane horses do, including black, bronze, chestnut, grey, and roan. An adult hippogriff's wingspan is approximately twenty-four feet. Hippogriffs are carnivorous and are extremely dangerous until tamed, which should only be attempted by a trained witch or wizard. That said, hippogriffs can and do live on insects, birds, and small animals such as rats and ferrets . A person wishing to approach a hippogriff should maintain eye contact and should bow first; if the animal bows in return, it can be touched and even ridden. Hippogriff owners are required to keep them under Disillusionment Charms to prevent Muggles from seeing them.

ILLEGAL OR 'IMPOSSIBLE'

✦ Flying car

Enchanting any Muggle object to fly is illegal, unless it's a broomstick. This law was written by the Misuse of Muggle Artifacts Office, which was run at the time by Arthur Weasley. Arthur carefully wrote a loophole into the law, however, which didn't make it illegal to enchant the item to fly if the witch or wizard had no intention of actually flying it, and then proceeded to enchant an old Ford Anglia to make it fly, giving it an invisibility booster just in case. Fred, George and Ron rescued Harry from the Dursleys' house using the car and a few weeks later Ron and Harry flew it to Hogwarts. Unfortunately, as they landed the car was badly damaged by an extremely violent tree, whereupon it ejected the boys from their seats in disgust and rumbled off to live in the forest.

◆ Flying carpet

Although flying carpets are used in other countries, currently they are banned in Britain. They're defined as Muggle artefacts, and are thus illegal to enchant.

◆ Flying wizard

Everyone thought that it wasn't possible for a witch or wizard to fly without some sort of device or object to help them; Lord Voldemort proved them wrong, however, when he flew unaided through the sky chasing Harry as the Order of the Phoenix was rescuing him from Privet Drive. Apparently he taught this magic to Snape as well.

APPENDIX TWO

In Search of
Grimmauld Place

by Tim Ledbetter (Ravenclaw Rambler)

✦

Number twelve, Grimmauld Place is the location of much of the action in Chapters 4 to 10 of *Harry Potter and the Order of the Phoenix*. It is Sirius Black's ancestral home, and the headquarters of the Order of the Phoenix. This essay discusses its possible location, and also that of the Ministry of Magic.

It has been suggested that Grimmauld Place is in the Tufnell Park area of north London, with which JKR was familiar. However, this is two-and-a-half miles from King's Cross railway station, and a passage at the beginning of OP10 makes it clear that King's Cross is only a twenty-minute walk away – for a large group encumbered by a lot of heavy luggage. This puts Grimmauld Place about a mile, or a bit less, from King's Cross. Grimmauld Place must therefore lie on a circle a little less than a mile in radius, with King's Cross at its centre.

What else do we know? Well, in OP7 we have a description of Harry and Mr. Weasley's journey by Underground to the Ministry of Magic. There are several very interesting points about this journey. Firstly, they walk along several streets to a 'miserable little underground station'. King's Cross is served by the Underground as well as the mainline station: indeed, with eight platforms, it is one of the biggest on the Underground network. Clearly King's Cross does not answer the description of the station used by Harry and Mr. Weasley. It is presumably more convenient to use this small station, rather than King's Cross, for the journey to the Ministry of Magic. Any location identified for Grimmauld Place must be consistent with a plausible reason for not taking the Underground from this station to go to King's Cross to catch the Hogwarts Express on September 1st.

Secondly, it is stated several times that the journey on the Underground takes Harry and Mr. Weasley to the very heart of London – therefore the station they go to is significantly more central than the station they started at. Moreover, at one point Mr. Weasley tells Harry that there are "four more stops" – indicating that they travel at least four stops, and probably more.

Finally, they arrive at a station which they leave by escalator. This is significant because in general only the deep-level tube lines built after 1890 have escalators. The Circle Line and the three other lines it shares tracks with date from mid-Victorian times, and were originally worked by steam trains, which of course needed ventilation to allow the steam to escape. They are much closer to the surface and their platforms are reached by ordinary stairs.

So, we are looking for somewhere rather insalubrious, a little less than one mile from King's Cross, whose nearest tube station is on a deep level tube line, and from which a journey of four stops or more on the Underground will take you to a station in central London. Note that the tube station itself may be more or less than twenty minutes' walk from King's Cross.

There are no less than fifteen stations on the London Underground within a mile of King's Cross: in alphabetical order they are Angel, Caledonian Road, Camden Town, Chancery Lane, Euston, Euston Square, Farringdon, Goodge Street, Great Portland Street, Highbury & Islington, Holborn, Mornington Crescent, Russell Square, Tottenham Court Road, and Warren Street. Let us see if we can narrow it down a bit.

Harry and Mr. Weasley travel "towards central London," so we can assume that they start from a station that is less central than their destination. Moreover, if they started too near the centre, a journey of four or more stops would take them out of the central area.

Let us perform an orbit of King's Cross, starting in the east, and working round clockwise.

Due east of King's Cross, a bit less than a mile away in Islington, is Angel Station, on the Northern Line. I think we can eliminate this one, as if you travel four stops north or south you will be heading away from the centre of London. Interestingly, on Pentonville Road, leading uphill from King's Cross to the Angel, there is a small park named after Joseph Grimaldi (1779–1837), the father of modern circus clowning, who was buried in this former churchyard. It would be nice to think of Grimaldi Park as being Grimmauld Place, but if it were, surely Harry and Mr Weasley would have used nearby King's Cross station in OP7, not a 'miserable little' one further away (and uphill).

South-east of King's Cross is Farringdon, on the Circle Line, and nearby is Chancery Lane, on the Central Line. These are both much too central: Chancery Lane in particular is in the centre of 'Lawyers' London' (Chancery is one of the divisions of the High Court). This seems to be an unlikely area to find Grimmauld Place. I have already explained why the Circle Line's absence of escalators at its stations makes that line unlikely, whilst if you travel four or more stops away from Chancery Lane you are heading away from the centre of London, and also rapidly run out of stations with escalators – many Central Line stations still use lifts.

To the south of King's Cross we have Holborn and Tottenham Court Road. Again, these are large stations, and are very central, so that travelling four or more stops from either of these would take you away from the centre of London.

Aldwych is an interesting possibility – definitely run down in the mid-1990s, and with a peak-hour-only service it could not have been used to go to King's Cross for 11am. Against it though, we find that it was extremely central, it was one end of a shuttle service to Holborn, so they would have to change there (people who count stops on the first leg of a tube journey on which they have to change trains, only count to the interchange station) and it closed in May 1994. This would put the dates in the canon out by at least two years since the date of Nearly Headless Nick's Deathday in CS8 gives the events in the early part of *Order of the Phoenix* as having taken place in August 1995.

A little closer to King's Cross lies Bloomsbury, served by Russell Square station, with Goodge Street a little further west. These are both quite small stations, near the edge of the central area, and travelling four stops south would take you to Piccadilly Circus or Embankment respectively, which are both very central. Goodge Street is of particular interest because the journey from Goodge Street to King's Cross would involve a change of trains, so it may be easier to walk rather than take the underground.

We now come to a collection of stations, on various lines, strung out close together along the Euston Road to the south west of King's Cross. Great Portland Street and Euston Square are on the Circle Line, and the same considerations as at Farringdon would seem to rule them out. Euston is a big Underground station – it serves a main line station bigger than King's Cross. Warren Street is a possibility – it is four stops from Charing Cross, the official centre of London, from which distances are measured, and at the end of Whitehall, where most Government Ministries are located – perhaps including the Ministry of Magic. However, Warren Street is on a direct line to King's Cross – if Grimmauld Place was near Warren Street, why did the party not use it to travel to King's Cross on September 1st?

West of King's Cross lies Mornington Crescent, famous from the BBC radio comedy show I'm Sorry I Haven't a Clue – the game Mornington Crescent has only one rule, which is that the players take turns to name a Tube station, and the first one to say "Mornington Crescent" is the winner! The station is small, not on a direct line to King's Cross, and four stops would take you to Tottenham Court Road, five to Leicester Square and six to Charing Cross, all of which are very central. This would be a most promising candidate except for the unfortunate circumstance that it was mothballed from 1992 to 1998, neatly bracketing the events in the early part of *Order of the Phoenix*, for which the canonical date is 1995, as I have already discussed.

About twenty minutes' walk north of King's Cross lies York Way station. This is definitely very run down, and would fit the bill almost perfectly except for the fact that it closed in 1932. If Harry and Mr Weasley used this station, we have to resolve a very large number of anomalies: Harry would have had to be born no later than 1917. Frank Bryce could have been injured in the Crimean War (or maybe the American Civil War), but the Ford Anglia appearing in *Chamber of Secrets* would have had to be fitted with a "flux capacitor" like the

DeLorean in *Back to the Future* (or perhaps a Time-Turner) as no Ford was badged as an Anglia until 1940! I think we'd better carry on looking!

There remain Camden Town, to the north-west of King's Cross, Caledonian Road, to the north, and Highbury & Islington to the north-east. As these are all rather further than a mile from King's Cross, Grimmauld Place would have to be some distance to the south of them to be only a twenty-minute walk from King's Cross. This actually supports them as possibilities, as it would explain why they were not used for the journey to King's Cross. (Another possible explanation is that Camden Town is "exit only" on Sunday mornings to reduce the crowds visiting Camden Market, so it could not have been used to travel to King's Cross to catch the Hogwarts Express at 11am on the day before term started – Hogwarts terms always seem to start on Mondays.) At the canonical date of 1995 the area had some seedy parts, although it has been largely "gentrified" in the subsequent ten years, and a large area was swept away for the construction of the new railway line connecting St. Pancras station to the Channel Tunnel. To see what it used to be like, watch the 1950s Ealing comedy *The Ladykillers*, much of which was filmed on location in this area.

Five stops from Highbury & Islington takes you to Green Park station: on the other side of the eponymous park lies Whitehall, the Muggle seat of government. Could this also be where the Ministry of Magic is to be found? It's possible, although the walk to the Ministry of Magic is said to be through the streets rather than a park.

More promisingly, five stops from either Caledonian Road (on the Piccadilly Line) or Camden Town (on the Northern Line) takes you to the intersection of those two lines at Leicester Square station, which is on the Charing Cross Road, where the Leaky Cauldron is to be found. Although distance is no object to wizards who can Apparate, it would make some kind of sense for the wizards' pub to be near the Ministry of Magic. One more stop down the Northern Line takes you to Charing Cross itself, at the northern end of Whitehall.

Grimmauld Place was therefore probably about three quarters of a mile from King's Cross, somewhere to the north of it, and closer to either Camden Town or Caledonian Road station than it is to

King's Cross. Consequently, the Ministry of Magic is probably near Leicester Square or Charing Cross stations, close to both the Leaky Cauldron and to the Muggle government ministries.

NOTES

The author gratefully acknowledges the contributions of George Scerbakov to the discussion of Angel Station and Grimaldi Park.

An alternative explanation as to why the day after the arrival at Hogwarts (2nd September) always seems to be a Monday is that Hogwarts may choose to operate a normal Monday timetable on the first day of term, regardless of what day of the week it actually is – just as my local railway company operates a Sunday service on Good Friday, and a church may have its usual Sunday services on festivals like Christmas and Ascension Day. Similar tinkering with the school calendar would help to explain a lot of date anomalies in the books, such as why there were lessons on Valentine's Day 1993 (which was a Sunday), or even how there could be two Mondays in a row.

[Editor's note: The 'two Mondays in a row' reference is to an error in GF that was corrected in later editions, and hence is not canon.]

© 2006 by Ravenclaw Rambler

Edited by Paula Hall and Michele Worley

APPENDIX THREE

In Search of
Little Whinging

by Tim Ledbetter (Ravenclaw Rambler)

✦

Where is Little Whinging? What sort of place did Harry Potter grow up in? The books in the canon give us several clues, mostly in Books 1 and 5 (*Philosopher's Stone* and *Order of the Phoenix*), but beware...there may be a red herring!

In Book 1, the first letter from Hogwarts (and presumably the others), is addressed to Harry in 'Little Whinging, Surrey.' Moreover, in Book 5, the charge sheet read out to Harry at the Wizengamot also identifies Little Whinging as being in Surrey. Other possibly relevant information is to be found later in Book 1, describing where Harry went after his visit to Diagon Alley on the afternoon of his eleventh birthday, and the description in Book 5 of the broomstick flight to Grimmauld Place, four years later.

Surrey is a county in England – the name is a corruption of 'South Region', from its location south of the River Thames, which divides it from London. The boundaries have changed over time, mainly as a result of the expansion of the conurbation of London. Surrey and Middlesex both lost territory to the new County of London in 1888, and again when 'Greater London' was formed in 1965. Middlesex ceased to exist as an administrative county in 1965: most of it became part of Greater London, but a small part in the extreme west, around Staines, was instead transferred to Surrey, giving that county territory north of the Thames for the first time. Minor boundary changes have also taken place more recently, particularly in the area of Heathrow Airport in 1994 and 1995.

First, we must recall that the identification of Surrey as the location of Little Whinging is given by the address on a letter (PS3). Official Post Office addresses still use the pre-1965 counties – thus a large swathe of Greater London, from Croydon round to Richmond, has Surrey postal addresses, but the area north of the Thames, around Staines, although administered as part of Surrey, still has Middlesex postal addresses. Although we cannot be sure that the wizard who addressed the letter would appreciate this distinction, we can, I think, be fairly sure that Uncle Vernon would have seized on any anomaly in the address on Harry's letter as evidence that the letter was not for him. Professor Dumbledore was no less astute than Uncle Vernon, and would have challenged any hint of an anomaly in the charges made against Harry at the Wizengamot in Book 5. Thus I think we can be sure that Little Whinging is in the postal county of Surrey, and is south of the Thames.

The next evidence I want to consider is the account of the broomstick ride in Book 5.

> "If they take out all of us and [only] you survive, Harry ... keep flying east..." He wondered how long they had been flying; it felt like an hour at least... "Time to start the descent!" ...They were heading for the largest collection of lights he had yet seen...
>
> (*Harry Potter and the Order of the Phoenix*, CHAPTER 3)

This last passage indicates that the lights of London only came into view towards the end of the ride, so there must be a significant distance between Little Whinging and the edge of the London conurbation. But how far, exactly? We must bear in mind that the flight time of an hour was only Harry's subjective impression. We have never been told the cruising speed of a broomstick, but as the rider is exposed to the elements (note the difficulty Harry has seeing when playing Quidditch in the rain, and the reference, during the broomstick ride itself, to Harry having to screw his eyes up against the rush of the wind) it cannot be much more than about 30 mph. However, for the lights of London to only come into view towards the end of the flight, the journey must have started some distance from London – it cannot have been much less than 30 miles. Given that

Surrey is only about 30 miles across, and lies to the south and west of London, this puts Little Whinging near the border with one of the neighbouring counties to the south or west: Sussex, Hampshire and Berkshire.

The directions given by Moody, together with Tonks's insistence that they do not double back, indicate that they were flying generally eastwards rather than northwards. We must therefore look to the western edge of the county, in or near the towns of Camberley, Frimley, or possibly Farnham. These are dormitory towns for London (I have already mentioned that they have regular train services to Waterloo station), and also support some light industry, like Vernon Dursley's drill company, Grunnings.

You cannot go far in Surrey without finding a street named for a plant of some kind – Mychett, between Camberley and Farnham, has both a Hazel Road and a Poplar Close, whilst Camberley itself has a Larchwood Glade, Lime Avenue, Maywood Drive, Chestnut Avenue, Linden Court and Amberwood Drive. Of the street names used in Little Whinging, there are several Magnolias in the Surrey street atlas (including a real Magnolia Close in Kingston-upon-Thames). There are many other streets named for shrubs (about twenty each named after Hazel, Laurel, Laburnum, and Poplar) in Surrey, but sadly I can find none named after either Privet or Wisteria (although both can be found in nearby Hampshire).

Incidentally, if Little Whinging is in the Camberley area, the zoo visited for Dudley's 11th birthday (PS2) is probably Marwell, near Winchester, in Hampshire: easily reached from the area using the M3 motorway. London Zoo is ruled out as until his visit with Hagrid 'Harry had never been to London before.' (PS5) Chessington Zoo, although in Surrey, is part of a theme park. If they had gone there, they would have had plenty of other things to do when 'Dudley had got bored of the animals by lunchtime.' (PS2)

But what of the evidence of Harry's return to the Dursleys, after his first visit to Diagon Alley, from Paddington railway station? (PS5) Here we have a problem, because no station in Surrey has had a direct train service from Paddington since the service to Richmond via Hammersmith was withdrawn in 1906. Nearly all railway stations in Surrey have direct services from London, but they all use either Waterloo or Victoria stations, both of which are more accessible from the Charing Cross Road than Paddington is. (Waterloo is three stops on the London Underground from Leicester Square station.)

Between the boundary changes of 1965 and 1995 the extreme northern tip of Surrey was Poyle, a suburb of Slough. After it lost its own branch line from Paddington in 1965, its nearest main line railway station became Langley, in Buckinghamshire, on the main Paddington to Reading line. But there are several difficulties with this. In particular: although Langley is indeed the nearest main line station to Poyle, the Heathrow terminus of London Underground's Piccadilly Line is nearer. That line calls at Leicester Square, which is on Charing Cross Road and therefore convenient for the Leaky Cauldron. If Little Whinging was in the Poyle area, Harry would surely have gone home that way.

Poyle has a Middlesex postal address, and by the time of the events in Book 5 the 1995 boundary change had transferred it from the administrative county of Surrey to that of Berkshire.

Poyle is too close to London to satisfy the description of the broomstick ride.

Harry may have changed trains at Reading, to get to Blackwater, Farnborough North, or North Camp, which are on a cross-country route with no direct service to London and all within yards of the Surrey/Hampshire border near Camberley and Frimley, although only North Camp is actually in Surrey. It is possible, but rather unlikely, that Harry might have chosen to travel to Privet Drive this way, if the circuitous journey via Paddington avoided a long walk to Privet Drive, encumbered as he was with all his purchases, or if the direct line from Waterloo was closed for some reason that day.

However, a much simpler explanation is possible. Let us look carefully at the antepenultimate paragraph of Chapter 5 of Book 1 – 'Hagrid helped Harry onto the train that would take him back to the Dursleys...,' (PS5) Note first the lack of an apostrophe – it is taking him, not necessarily to the Dursleys' (house), but to the Dursleys (the family). We have ample evidence in both Books 1 and 5 that Harry is not trusted in the house on his own – he would not have had to 'spoil' Dudley's birthday treat by going with them to the

Zoo, for a start – so he will not have been allowed a latchkey and could not go to Privet Drive unless the Dursleys were at home.

But have we any reason to suppose the Dursleys were NOT at home that afternoon? Well, yes! They were last seen that morning, shortly after midnight, retreating into the back room of the Hut-on-the-Rock (PS4). Since the boat was still there in the morning, they cannot have left before Harry and Hagrid. And since Hagrid took the boat, they cannot have left afterwards: not until somebody came to fetch them! Uncle Vernon had especially chosen the place for its lack of communication, so it would be difficult for the Dursleys to summon help. And no-one, apart from Harry and Hagrid, knew they were there.

So Harry couldn't go to Privet Drive after his visit to Diagon Alley – first he had to go 'back to the Dursleys' to get them off the Hut-on-the-Rock. And so his train from Paddington was not taking him to Little Whinging at all!

© 2006 by Ravenclaw Rambler

Edited by Paula Hall and Michele Worley

INDEX

✦

The Orkneys

Isle of Skye
Loch Ness
✦ INVERNESS

GLENFINNAN
FORT
WILLIAM
Rannoch Station
✦ RANNOCH
MOOR
Duart Castle
ISLE OF MULL
S C O T L A N D

GLASGOW ✦
✦ EDINBURGH

✦ NEWCASTLE UPON TYNE

Ingleton ✦
YORKSHIRE
MOORS

LEEDS ✦
✦ KINGSTON UPON HULL

LIVERPOOL ✦
New Mills
MANCHESTER ✦
✦ SHEFFIELD

✦ NOTTINGHAM

E N G L A N D

✦ BIRMINGHAM

W A L E S

CARDIFF ✦
Bristol ✦
Langley and Iver ✦
London
Wiltshire
Camberley ✦
Surrey

BRIGHTON

Shebbear ✦
EXMOOR
Quoditch ✦
Exeter ✦
Ottery St Mary ✦
Hangleton
CHUDLEIGH ✦ BUDLEIGH SALTERTON
Tintagel ✦
Dartmoor ✦ TEIGNMOUTH
BODMIN
MOOR
✦ PLYMOUTH